Gentle Wisdom

for

Tough Times

Stories of High Adventure and Raw Faith

Mary Dunham Faulkner

evangeline
press

Gentle Wisdom For Tough Times
Published by Evangeline Press

© 2003 by Evangeline Press and Mary Dunham Faulkner
International Standard Book Number: 0-9728048-1-1

Cover design by Data & Graphic Solutions

All Scripture quotations, unless otherwise indicated,
are the author's paraphrase of commonly known verses in *The Holy Bible*.

Scripture quotations marked AMPLIFIED are taken from The Amplified ® Bible,
Copyright © 1954, 1958, 1962, 1965, 1987 by the Lockman Foundation. Published by
Zondervan Publishing House. Used by permission. (www.Lockman.org)

Scripture quotations marked KJV are taken from the King James Version of the Bible.

Scripture quotations marked NIV are taken from *The Holy Bible*, New International
Version ®. Copyright © 1973, 1978, 1984 by International Bible Society.
Used by permission of Zondervan Publishing House. All rights reserved.
The "NIV" and "New International Version" trademarks are registered
in the United States Patent and Trademark Office by International Bible Society.

Scripture quotations marked NKJV are taken from the New King James Version. Copyright
© 1879, 1980, 1982 by Thomas Nelson, Inc. Used by permission. All rights reserved.

Scripture quotation marked PHILLIPS is from J.B. Phillips, The New Testament in
Modern English. Copyright © 1960 by J. B. Phillips. Printed in Great Britain by Cox &
Wyman Ltd., Reading for the publishers Geoffrey Bles Ltd., 52 Doughty Street, London,
WC1. Used by permission. All rights reserved.

First Printing May 2004
Second Printing February 2005
Third Printing May 2008

Requests for information should be addressed to:
Evangeline Press, P O Box 17-1234, Irving, TX 75017-1234
Printed in Colombia

To the memory of Jake,
whose steady walk, extravagant love and
outrageous humor made him a favorite brother,
in our hearts forever.

Acknowledgements

Mt. Hermon is a writer's sanctuary, tucked away in the California hills where the combination of tranquility, beauty, and the possibility of a Barnes and Nobles blockbuster draws wannabe writers, published authors, and seeking editors from around the nation. It was during one of these weeks of intense interaction, that I met Elaine Wright Colvin, a published author, editor and writing instructor…and as it turns out, a woman sent by God to me.

Ruthlessly honest (do you want me to make you feel good or do you want me to tell you the truth?) and compassionately encouraging, she has dogged me every year asking, "What are you working on now, Mary?" And "When can I see your new manuscript?" She believed that I was a writer (long before I was absolutely sure) and in this book (long before it was finished) and kept telling me that it would be published, that it would be beautiful, that it would impact many people. I believed her, which shows you the power of having even one balcony person in your life. Thank you, Elaine.

Nobody wants to admit that they are not as accomplished as they want to be, but I must thank Paula Rowland, a true professional, who re-checked facts, dates, and the wrong use of a comma. I am honored to have worked with such a ruthlessly detail oriented woman who made me "go over it one more time." Tara Goodman, a talented wordsmith took the rough copy and cleaned it up, making me look good in the process. And Judy Fisher, who, like God, creates and makes all things beautiful. Thank you.

Kim Arnold has been a force behind this small work, cheering and working behind the scenes to make sure it saw the light of day. Thank you, Kim. May your kind multiply and fill the earth.

And finally, to my husband, Joe Faulkner, a natural born encourager who gifted me with a laptop and a charge to use it: "Mary, you're a writer. Write." Thank you for always cheering me on to my next victory. I'm glad I'm on your team.

Contents

— Part Three —
Gaining Wisdom Through Signing Up For Service

— Conclusion —
Enduring to the End

Momma had eleven children and a demanding husband whose needs always came first in our household. Finding a few moments in a day when we children had her undivided attention was a rare and wonderful treat. As siblings, we were used to sharing everything: toys, baths, beds—and mom. We all developed our own set of personal tricks to get her all to our self. Getting sick, being bad or uncommonly good all worked well, but I usually reserved my best shot for bedtime.

"Tell me a story," I wheedled, trying to draw out those delicious moments when dinner was over, the dishes done, and the house quiet. After we went to sleep, Mother would be at the ironing board, attacking the mountain of clothes that never seemed to diminish, or giving the kitchen floor one last "lick and a promise." But for now, she was mine. Well, almost, because none of us had the luxury of having our own bedroom, or even sleeping alone. I squeezed between warm bodies to be the one closest to her on the bed.

Her name was CeCelia Evangeline, but her identity was swallowed up in mothering. Even Daddy called her "Momma" (and she called him "Daddy" until the day he died). She was short and round and soft and reminded me of a lioness whose fur was thick and pliant, but whose belly was filled with a formidable power. She never roared, but we were all aware of Momma's strength. She kept the household and our world moving on its axis.

Daddy was a disciplinarian, hard and unyielding at times, but with all of his authority, he never had the long-haul-kind-of-strength of Momma.

It didn't matter if it was a good or bad kind-of-day, she handled them all

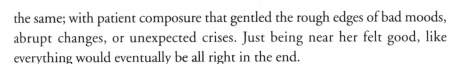

the same; with patient composure that gentled the rough edges of bad moods, abrupt changes, or unexpected crises. Just being near her felt good, like everything would eventually be all right in the end.

It never dawned on me to ask Mother to read a fairy tale to us. Why would she? There was not a book anywhere that could compete with the real life stories she told of Tibet, China, Africa; having babies at home instead of a hospital; outwitting robbers; or conquering life-debilitating illnesses. I closed my eyes and her words were my first movies, splashed across my imagination with colorful details that gave drama and depth to the backdrop of her scenes.

"When I washed the diapers in the ice-cold Tibetan stream, my arms ached all the way up to my elbows" she said, and I could see the snowdrifts on each side of the stream, her breath smoking up the atmosphere, her hands red-raw from rubbing clothes in freezing temperatures.

When she described the donkey that carried her and her baby over the steep mountain range, I held my breath envisioning the sheer drop-offs on either side of them, and I snuggled closer to her, marveling that she was safe. She was the heroine in each adventure and I couldn't imagine anyone smarter, stronger, or braver than Momma.

We never had a television in our home, so I don't know what it was like for other families who gathered around a TV instead of being squashed together in a bed listening to the latest continuing saga that sometimes took days to finish.

Sometimes Momma would doze off, succumbing to the combination of a soft bed and the miracle of completely quiet children. Her sentences would trail off into winding repetitions and finally end in unfinished cliff hangers. Then she would awaken to our cries of, "…and then what happened?"

I learned about life from Momma's stories: how to enjoy the adventure of life, how to respect the fact that life is fragile and full of the unexpected. Tucked away in every escapade were seeds of a theology that have stood the test of time for me: Trust God in every situation, don't make the answers complicated, nor the formula complex; if you're squabbling ask for forgiveness; if you're guilty, repent; if you're in trouble, pray.

When Mother turned ninety, she went to the doctor for a check-up and was stunned with the test results: She had cancer of the uterus. To Mother, it was the unthinkable. A nurse and a preacher's wife, she had sat at the bedside of many terminally ill patients, helping them through the long pain-filled days and nights.

"Not cancer," she grieved the news. "I don't mind dying, I just don't want to die of cancer."

I watched Mother walk through another crisis, maybe her final one. It was the kind that had the possibility of another good story when the ending was tacked on. But for now, watching her was anguish. She was taking one of those journeys that must be made alone and I could only imagine the fierce battle she was waging against fear. She seemed frail and small and I wished it appropriate to hold her and take the pain away as she had done for me so many times.

After a few days of silent grief, she woke up one morning happy, and dressed for breakfast.

"Well, what happened to *you*?" I asked, delighted but confused at the abrupt change in her mood.

"I woke up in the middle of the night and couldn't sleep because I was so tormented with the thought of cancer. After tossing and turning and crying, I cried out to God and asked him, 'God! What am I going to do?' You know, I heard Him say very clearly, 'Don't worry. We'll do this together.' If He is going to do this with me, then I can do it." Her statement was matter of fact. Settled.

I marveled at how quickly Mother found her peace, and again through the following months and years, how she kept it. She didn't speak of cancer again, prayed that God would heal her, and assumed He did.

Two years later, I was out at the ranch where she lived, taking my turn sitting with her during her final bed-ridden days. Her body was fragile—and unutterably precious—like one of grandma's old teacups. I caressed her paper thin arms and practiced small moments of letting her go. When the visiting nurse came out to check on her, I stepped outside the house to ask for details of Momma's progress. "Does the cancer seem to be worse?" I queried.

"Cancer? There's nothing in her records that indicates she has cancer and I can't see any signs of it. She's simply old and wearing out."

I smiled, happy that Mother had won her final round. She had refused to live out her final years in torment or fear. Yes, she was simply old and "wearing out." But her faith was unyielding, strong. She had left me with one last faith adventure that had an ending just like the others. It doesn't matter what you face, even cancer, old age, and finally death, "If Jesus does it with you, you can do it."

PART ONE

GAINING WISDOM
THROUGH GETTING STARTED

CHAPTER ONE

Wisdom Is... Taking the First Step

How do you know you are called into the ministry? Maybe it is different for other people, but for Daddy and me, we knew we were called because we had no desire to do anything else. From the very beginning, right after we came to know the Lord, our great passion was to pray and preach and spread the gospel. It seemed like the most natural decision in the world.

In fact, right after Daddy accepted Christ into his life, he prayed, "Lord, I want to be a missionary and preach the gospel, but I don't know where to go, or how to begin. Lord, I don't even have a car."

There's a forty-foot wide highway in front of you. What's stopping you? Daddy told me later that these words were strong thoughts in his spirit. Was this the Holy Spirit speaking to him? He wasn't sure, but if it was, he wasn't about to ignore Him.

"Momma, would you be willing to start walking down the road to preach the gospel?" he asked me.

"Well, uh…uh…" I stalled for time while I let the idea race through my mind. *Walk down the road? Just start walking?* I had told the Lord I would go anywhere; do anything for Him, but whoever heard of just walking down the road? We had a baby girl to take care of, and we had no money, no car, and no job. I knew if I told Daddy that I wouldn't go, he would accuse me of not wanting to do the will of God. But if I told him yes, then I would have to do it. *How should I answer him?*

I thought of my staid Norwegian mother and how shocked and dismayed she would be to know her daughter and granddaughter were living like vagabonds and ragamuffins. Would I be able to hurt her like that? And how about my baby daughter, what kind of life would that be for her?

Still, I knew that I wanted to do the will of God as much as Daddy did. If God told him to go down the highway, then that was also the will of God for me.

"Daddy, if you are sure that God said to start walking down the highway, then I'll walk with you," I told him. That's all he needed to know. From that day on, we made preparations for our new life.

The first thing we had to do was to get rid of all our things…which weren't a whole lot. We were poor and just getting started, but we still had too much to carry down the road, that's for sure. I started giving everything away that we could not put in one suitcase. Another small suitcase would be for the baby's diapers. I didn't mind so much about my things, but I hated giving away the baby's things. She had a nice little stroller, but it couldn't be folded up and so I gave it away. Her beautiful pink and blue baby blanket that

Pews, even empty ones, would have been easier to face than that long stretch of highway before us.

I was so proud of wouldn't fit in the suitcase so it had to go too. I was glad she was not old enough to know I was giving away her things—one of us feeling bad about it was enough.

I'll never forget that first day that Daddy and I officially entered "the ministry." Pews, even empty ones, would have been easier to face than that long stretch of highway before us. Our little family started walking together with me holding the baby, Juanita, and Daddy carrying the two suitcases. An hour hadn't passed before I realized that this was not going to be easy…my legs were already tired from walking and my arms ached from carrying the baby.

I didn't complain but Daddy must have sensed my feelings. "Momma, some day you and I are going to have our own Cadillac," he said, no doubt trying to comfort me. I laughed out loud. "Cadillac?" We couldn't even afford a jalopy.

You know, he was right. In later years, we always drove a Cadillac. We needed a large, dependable car for our large family and Cadillacs were the best solution for our needs. But back then, I would have been thankful for a bicycle. It was so discouraging to look up ahead and see miles and miles of never-ending hot, black asphalt.

We had decided not to raise a hand or thumb to ask for a ride. If we were going to live a life of faith, we would start practicing it on this highway...

We had decided not to raise a hand or thumb to ask for a ride. If we were going to live a life of faith, we would start practicing it on this highway, right now. We prayed every morning before we set out, asking God to provide for us and choose our drivers. In return, we promised Him that we would share the gospel with anyone who picked us up. Every ride provided us with an opportunity to witness to our driver. All we had to do was to answer the questions everyone always asked:

"Where are you going?"

"We don't know yet. We're following the will of God."

"What do you mean?"

And then we would be off, telling them about the plan of salvation, eternity, and the need to follow and obey God. Yes, I know it sounds crazy, but it worked.

One day it started raining and there wasn't a car in sight. The baby was getting wet even though I had covered her with a blanket. My legs and arms were tired and I was discouraged. What if no one picked us up? What were we doing anyway? We didn't have a home anywhere in the world and all of us were hungry. I was wet and tired and scared that there would be more days like this one. I started crying with fatigue and fear. I tried to pray with faith, but what came out was more like a complaint. "Lord, look at us. We need you. We have nothing: no home, no car, and no food. Please help us."

Within minutes I heard the distant rumble of a ten-wheeler coming down the road behind us. I held my breath, still praying. You could always tell if they were going to stop by the sound of the motor. Screeching brakes never sounded so sweet in all of my life. Once the truck stopped, Daddy pulled himself up on the sideboard and opened the door to find a big, burly truck driver who thankfully had a soft heart.

"The wife and baby can go upstairs," he motioned up over his head. "Upstairs" was a cubicle above the front seat with just enough room to sleep one person. I crawled up there, hugging my baby to me, weak with relief that we were safe and warm and dry. I didn't even know where we were going or how long it would take us to get there. But for this moment everything was well. We were still hungry, but at least we could have a nice, long rest.

Later, I woke up to find we had stopped in front of a restaurant.

"Would you like to have something to eat?" the driver asked.

"O Yes! That would be great!" Daddy and I both spoke at the same time. I'm sure he could tell we were hungry by the excitement in our voices."

After our meal, we stayed in the town and walked over to the Assembly of God church. We stayed for their Wednesday night service and worshiped with people we had never met but who treated us as if we were family.

"Do you have a place to stay tonight?" the minister asked us. When we told him that we didn't, he immediately took us to a nearby hotel and checked us in.

"Lord, this is wonderful," I prayed in my heart. A nice soft bed with clean sheets seemed like heaven to me. Never mind that we didn't know what we were going to do or where we would go tomorrow. We didn't even have money for breakfast, but God was taking care of us today. I knew if I was going to make it I would have to learn to have faith for one day at a time.

"Oh by the way," the preacher turned around as he was walking away, "Here's two dollars for breakfast."

We went to bed feeling like kings without a care in the world. Our simple faith in God's ability to care for our every need was as small as a mustard seed, but it was already growing. We were learning lessons that couldn't be found in seminary textbooks, only in real life.

To outsiders, I'm sure we looked foolish. Even today some would call us naive to believe that by striking out on the highway without financial support was the will of God.

Well, perhaps we were foolish. But it was the right way for us. Since the beginning, we have always believed that trusting God for everything was the only way to live. Now maybe that's a simple way to live. But it worked for me for the seventy years I've lived since that day.

That one highway eventually led us to nations we never dreamed we would live in and to people and cultures we never knew we would minister to. The faith that we needed to believe God would provide transportation, food, and shelter; was the same faith we needed to survive danger in Tibet, bombing in China, and malaria in Africa.

And it all began with one step on a forty-foot wide highway.

For most of us, leaving the familiar and safe is usually the hardest decision we will ever make. Doing something we've never done before goes against our natural desire to feel secure. But that's the only way we're going to get moving on our journey. We have to take that first step.

Hearing God's voice isn't hard. If we listen, we can hear Him talking to us. Obeying what He says is the hard part. Learning to trust God with that first step is contrary to our carnal natures, but it is also the only way to see what great things He has in store for our lives.

"By faith Abraham, when called to go to a place he would later receive as his inheritance, obeyed and went, even though he did not know where he was going. By faith he made his home in the promised land like a stranger in a foreign country; he lived in tents...For he was looking forward to the city with foundations, whose architect and builder is God." (Hebrews 11: 8, 10)

Chapter Two

Wisdom is...Believing God is Enough

The very first time we started preaching was a few days after we began walking down the road in faith. The first truck driver who picked us up let us off in Billings, Montana; so we figured that Billings, Montana was the place we were supposed to start working for God. But where? We found a little store front church that had a sign saying it was a church, but there were no lights on inside.

"Let's start singing," Daddy said. I looked around, hoping no one was watching while we sang every Christian song we knew. It was obvious that I was going to have to get rid of all of my pride if I was going to follow Jesus and John Dodge. It wasn't long before the pastor came outside, a woman who seemed happy to meet us and especially to know that we were Christians. We introduced ourselves and told her that we were following God into the ministry.

"Can you preach?" she asked Daddy.

"Yes," Daddy said without blinking an eye.

It sure wasn't a very long interview, but he must have answered correctly, because we were offered our first official ministry opportunity right on the spot.

"If you will stay here and preach, I'll provide the board and room for your family. I can't give you money, but I have a boarding house and you will have a place to stay and something to eat as long as you stay here."

Board and room! I could have leapt for joy. This was the very first stop on our adventure and God was there ahead of time providing a roof over our heads and food to eat. It was one of the happiest days of our lives because we knew God was with us and was taking care of us.

Now the real test was, could Daddy preach?

We moved our two suitcases into the back room of the church and began to pray for the services the next night. Would anyone come? Would Daddy be able to say anything that would help them? I don't know who was more nervous, Daddy or I, but both of us started to fast and pray, asking God to use us.

We had three people the first night. One of them was mentally-ill or demon-possessed and kept seeing things. The other one was a little old man who also seemed very strange or drunk, and the third one was the pastor. I didn't know who to feel the most sorry for, Daddy for having to preach to such a strange congregation, or the strange congregation for having to listen to a brand new preacher who had more zeal than knowledge. As it turned out, we were a well-matched group. The pastor liked what Daddy had to say…or maybe she was just desperate…but either way she urged us to stay on.

We stayed in Billings for forty-nine days and preached in the storefront church every night for the whole time. Word of the nightly services spread through the town and our congregation began to grow. Daddy preached as hard and as long as he could every night. When he had nothing more to say, he gave an altar call. When people came forward to pray, he didn't know what to say to them, so he knelt down together with them and prayed himself. In spite of our ignorance, people were saved.

We were taking simple baby steps into our walk of faith; learning to trust God for everything—food, clothing, and even a place to stay. During the entire time we were there, we received one offering, and although it was only two dollars, our needs were supplied.

When we felt it was time to leave, we went back out on the highway and started hitchhiking again. This time we went to Denver. When our driver dropped us off, the first thing we did was ask everyone we met if they knew if there was a revival meeting in town. There was and we followed directions to a small Pentecostal church where the singing and worship was loud and lively. We were hungry for fellowship and wanted to learn as much as we could from believing Christians.

Of course we had no money and no place to stay. But our faith was built up by our last experience in Montana, and we were just sure God would provide. So far, He had used Christians to help us without our asking, so we just expected that this would happen again. When no one invited us home after the meeting we started to worry. *What were we going to do?* I could tell Daddy was wavering. We had never had to ask anyone for food or a place to stay yet, but it was almost midnight and we had no place to sleep. We were standing right next to a swank hotel, The Savoy, in downtown Denver and decided to go in and sit in the lobby while we decided what to do next.

"I hate to do it, but I guess we will have to ask the Salvation Army if they can put us up," Daddy said finally deciding. I don't know if it was his pride or his faith that was hurt most but we both hated asking for a handout, but it seemed we had no choice.

...both of us decided that if God could provide drivers and hotels and food, then surely He could provide a car.

Daddy asked the man behind the counter if he could help us find the number to the Salvation Army and he nodded and then disappeared into a back room. When he came back to the counter he had a big smile on his face and said, "Follow me." He took us in the elevator up to the eleventh floor where he unlocked a beautiful, luxurious room and said, "You can stay here tonight with us."

Just like that! Why, the carpet was so plush we would have been grateful just to sleep on the floor. But instead we were living like the rich people uptown. Before he closed the door behind him he said, "When you're ready for breakfast, just let us know and it will be on us, too."

God was teaching us lessons in guidance and faith that we would have never learned anywhere else.

After a couple of years of hitchhiking, both of us decided that if God could provide drivers and hotels and food, then surely He could provide a car. So, we asked Him for a car and went down to a car lot the next day to pick one out. Never mind that we didn't have any money. We figured that if you asked God for something and believed He would give it to you, then you just did the next thing. The next thing was to go looking for cars.

Daddy found a Model T he liked. It only cost fifty dollars, but for us it might as well have been 50,000 dollars. He asked the salesman if he could make payments of five dollars a month on it. Miraculously the salesman agreed.

It seemed that Model T was only worth about fifty dollars. We had planned to travel all over the States and evangelize in it. But it broke down one day not long after we bought it and we pushed it back to the nearest gas station. The radiator was smoking hot and Daddy poured water on it, thinking it was the logical thing to do to cool it down. Instead, he cracked the engine block. Now the car was ruined and we had no money to repair it.

> *...I should have known that you would have to do a lot more to Daddy than laugh at him to get him to back down.*

What were we going to do now? I felt like sitting down and crying right there. Hadn't God provided a miracle for us to get this car in the first place? So why would this happen to us now?

"Come on, Momma," Daddy had already started walking over to a used car lot. He asked to see the cheapest car they had. I thought he was crazy because I knew he only had one dollar and ten cents in his pocket. The salesman showed him a Buick for three hundred dollars and Daddy offered him five dollars a month with no down payment.

"I'm sorry, sir, I can't do that," the salesman nearly laughed in his face.

I could have told him that, I thought to myself and turned to leave, thinking the matter had been settled for us. But I should have known that you would have to do a lot more to Daddy than laugh at him to get him to back down.

"I want to speak to the manager," I heard him tell the salesman.

"If you insist," the smirk on his face belied his polite words. He knew it would do no good and I agreed with him.

When the manager came out of his office, Daddy offered him the same deal, five dollars a month with no down payment.

"Well, you'll have to pay for the fee to change the title. But yes, we can do that."

"How much is the title?" Daddy asked. I was holding my breath. We wouldn't even be able to buy a title, much less a car, but Daddy was acting like he had all the money in the world.

"One dollar and ten cents," was the reply.

Daddy handed over the last penny in his pocket, all the while acting like he had another couple of hundred to go with it. Both of us could have jumped up and down and shouted at the same time. And it wasn't just because we were driving a new car off the car lot. We were discovering that where God guides, He also provides.

In later years we would trust him for thousands of dollars and see marvelous miracles of provision. But that three hundred dollar Buick and the title that went with it was like a personal telegram from heaven telling us that we were on the right track, that God was with us and would take care of us. What more did we need?

Our complete trust is the greatest gift we can give to God. When we refuse to fret and worry over the unexpected needs in our life, we are worshipping Him, declaring that He is unlimited in His ability and creative power. After all, imagine the God we serve—who creates the universe, remains firmly in control over heaven and earth, and yet does not allow one sparrow to fall to the ground without His consent. Trust is born out of knowing three things about God: one, that He watches over the details of our lives; two, that He wants to be involved; and three, that He has all the power and resources of heaven and earth at His disposal to supply all that we need. God is enough.

"Are not two sparrows sold for a copper coin? And not one of them falls to the ground apart from your Father's will. But the very hairs of your head are all numbered. Do not fear therefore; you are of more value than many sparrows." (Matthew 10: 29 – 31)

CHAPTER THREE

Wisdom is...Listening to the Comforter

After Daddy discovered he could preach, he never wanted to do anything else. If there was an invitation to speak anywhere, he just automatically figured that God wanted him to do it. While traveling in Missouri, we visited a small Baptist church and ended up staying for several months because the people liked his preaching.

"If you stay here and help us, you can stay in the room in the back of the church," they offered.

Well, that was it for me. A room of our very own! It seemed too good to be true. We had been on the road without a place of our own for months and I was longing to nest somewhere, anywhere.

It was wintertime though and the snow came right through the cracks in the walls and made a little white patch on our bed. We were freezing cold and hungry. The offerings were usually only a dollar, or sometimes five, and never lasted the whole week. Daddy would go down by the railroad tracks and gather coal for the little pot bellied stove inside the church which helped keep us warm. We couldn't afford to eat balanced meals, so we bought small little loaves of bread and cocoa. I boiled water on top of the pot-bellied stove and made cocoa and we dipped our bread in it. It may not have been the most nutritious meal, but it filled and warmed our stomachs.

When the church people realized we didn't have very much food, they began to bring us turnips and greens. And every day we ate turnips and greens and drank cocoa. Our diet may have been a little more rounded because of the vegetables, but I was so sick of eating turnips I didn't care if I ever saw another one in my life.

When one of the women invited us over for dinner, both Daddy and I were excited. We were finally going to eat a balanced meal! I could just envision some fried chicken or a pot roast... and wouldn't it be wonderful if she fixed some mashed potatoes and gravy!

When we sat down to eat, I could have cried. There, right in the middle of the table, was a huge bowl of fresh, hot turnip greens. I'm sure it was all she could afford and neither Daddy nor I thought about complaining. At least to her. When we got home we comforted each other over having our dreams dashed and then laughed at how we had prepared ourselves for a feast.

That's probably the poorest we have been in our whole lives, but both of us were young and eager to follow the Lord. We were sure God had called us and just figured everyone in ministry lived this way.

Those were difficult days and while I knew God was caring for us, at times I became weary with the freezing cold, the empty cupboards, and the demands of ministry. One morning, I woke up missing my mother. I laid in bed for an extra ten minutes reveling in the memories of growing up on a farm where food was plentiful. I closed my eyes and could see the family's large two-story house with the beautiful hardwood floors and the cozy, crackling fire that took the sting out of Montana's harsh winters. I could almost smell mama's biscuits and see the rows of canned fruit and vegetables in our large pantry.

What had made me choose this kind of life? The longer I laid there, the more frustrated and angry I became. When I finally got up and heated the water for our morning cocoa, I was in such a dark mood I felt like throwing the few, cracked dishes that we had across the room.

Daddy was getting on his coat to go pray for a poor, sick woman who lived in a boxcar near the railroad track.

"Come on, Momma, we need to go,"

"No, I don't want to go and pray for anyone," I told him.

"Well, you have to go," Daddy insisted. "She's a woman living by herself and it wouldn't look right for me to go alone."

I would go, I decided, but I didn't have to pray. Nobody could make me pray if I didn't want to. I bundled up my bad mood and trudged through the snow over to the railroad tracks, following Daddy inside of a narrow little boxcar.

I had never met anyone who actually lived in part of a train before. I found myself looking at a gaunt, sick woman with long black hair lying on a bed near a pot-bellied stove in the middle of the "room." When I saw the pain on her face and her poor living conditions, my heart broke and I forgot about my bad mood, the family farm, and mother. She was why I wanted to be in ministry.

I walked over to her to pray for her and before I could say anything she put out her arms and hugged me and began praying for me. Her long, matchstick arms felt like the arms of God to me and I relaxed, cocooned in a strong, powerful love that washed over me in waves of pure joy.

So this was what the Holy Spirit felt like! I was so happy I pulled away from her and began to dance right there in that stark, black box car. I danced around and around the pot-bellied stove with my eyes shut and my hands raised into the air, never once touching that stove or getting burned. I felt like I was walking on air and that every heartache and burden had fallen off my shoulders. I was caught up in the most inexpressible joy and delight and kept saying

I felt like I was walking on air and that every heartache and burden had fallen off my shoulders.

over and over again, "Jesus reigns in heaven and all is well." The message didn't start in my mind, which was depressed and disgruntled moments before, but rather erupted out of my spirit.

When we left that poor little woman I felt like the richest woman in the world. Deep in my spirit, more than ever before, I knew that Jesus reigns. In my innocence, I thought this meant that I would never have any more problems again in my life. I had tasted of the most wonderful joy I had ever known. How could anything be bad again after this?

I was too young in the Lord to know that the Holy Spirit is given to us, for just that reason—because life has many heartaches and crushing problems. Since that day in the boxcar, I have spent my days becoming more intimate with the Comforter.

In fact, in the years that have followed, Daddy and I had ten more children, traveled the world, and passed through what seemed like endless valleys where the circumstances were as dark as the black, chipped paint on that railroad car. Those are the times that I have learned to reach up for the Holy Spirit's comfort and strength by remembering the powerful revelation I received that day. In fact, I have quoted the words to my children (and now to their children) whenever I think they are in danger of forgetting; Jesus reigns in heaven and all is well.

God knew that you and I could not make it through this life without the soft comfort and strong guidance of the Holy Spirit. The Comforter always points us to Jesus and reminds us that no matter what we are walking through, He is there with us. Our spirits receive strength and courage, able to withstand any onslaught from Satan when we are fused in intimacy with the Holy Spirit. He is constantly speaking to us, telling us that Jesus reigns and all is well. The question is, are we listening?

"However when He, the Spirit of truth has come, He will guide you into all truth; for He will not speak on His own authority, but whatever He hears He will speak; and He will tell you things to come. He will glorify Me, for He will take of what is Mine and declare it to you. All things that the Father has are Mine. Therefore I said that He will take of Mine and declare it to you." (John 16: 13 – 15)

CHAPTER FOUR

Wisdom Is...Seeing God in Everything

How in the world did a proper Norwegian girl end up hitchhiking her way into the ministry? Thank God, my mother couldn't see me now. The long, never-ending highways Daddy and I were traveling on were miles away from the happy, carefree days of my childhood.

Those were the days when my five brothers and sisters and I lived on our family's thousand-acre ranch under the big skies of Montana. It was a different life, a different time. No one had heard of day care centers or of mothers having careers for that matter. Everybody knew that women stayed home and took care of the children while the men worked to make a living. That's just the way it was. We didn't have as many choices as women do today, but then our lives were simpler.

We were a family of full-blooded Norwegians surrounded by a community rooted in a heritage of God and family. Our neighbors were people like us who had homesteaded the Northwest plains, where anyone could stake out land and make a living if they were willing to sacrifice and work hard.

The men left for the fields early in the morning and spent the day coaxing the land to give up its harvest, which for us were acres and acres of wheat. Now just because the women stayed home didn't mean they didn't work. We had to get up before the men did to start breakfast: flapjacks and eggs, steak and ham, oatmeal and biscuits. There was so much food that had to be prepared that it was like cooking for a small cafeteria. After we did the dishes, milked the cows, and worked the garden, we had to start all over again to prepare lunch and dinner. Nobody ever went to a restaurant to eat. Why, you just didn't think about it. But I can tell you we were a lot healthier than people are today.

Once a week my sisters and I washed our clothes by hand, hung them out to dry, brought them in, folded, ironed, and put them away. Mother insisted on a clean house with shiny wood floors, dusted corners, and scrubbed down cupboards. Besides that, we had to make sure our supply of canned vegetables and fruit was going to be enough for the cold winter months when the garden was dormant. That meant picking, pulling, and chopping fruits and vegetables for hours until you thought your arm was going to break. Big black pots of simmering beans and potatoes, peaches and apricots were poured into sterilized jars and sealed for the winter. Whoever said that a woman's work is never done must have lived on our farm for a while.

It may have been a harder life, but sometimes easier is not better.

My grandchildren can't imagine a life like that. "Grandma, it sounds like you didn't have much fun," one of them commented after I described a normal day on the farm. "Why, we always had fun," I tell them. And we sure didn't need a TV or Internet to entertain us. It may have been a harder life, but sometimes easier is not better.

Supper was the time when we relaxed every evening. Work was over, the day was almost done, and everyone seemed to be in a better mood than at breakfast. It was the time we sat around our big dinner table in one of the newest, nicest homes on the prairie and enjoyed the fruit of all the hard work: home-made biscuits, Norwegian meat balls and gravy, and fresh vegetables from the garden. No one was in a hurry to leave the table and so we sat and laughed at each other's stories, told jokes, and discussed what was happening in the community.

Every now and then, we would gather the horses and hitch them to our buggy and ride into town or go to a neighbor's house (which was always miles away) for a special dinner. I remember the frigid winter nights, when Mother would heat up bricks to keep our feet warm and put a blanket over us to help shield us from the wind. Later, my Dad bought the first motorcar in our community, which created news for miles around. Not many people could afford one and I was proud of my hard-working family and a father who knew how to manage his money. He always took good care of us.

I have always been closer to my Dad who was good-natured and fun. Mother was the disciplinarian of the family and made sure we all did what we were supposed to do, but Dad was always happy and easy to talk to. Sometimes, after a hard week of work, he and Mother would invite our neighbors and friends for dinner and square dancing. They came from miles around and danced into the early morning hours. Dad always danced one or two dances with me first and then sent me

Mother knew how badly I wanted to be a nurse and encouraged me every step of the way.

to bed along with the other kids. Of course dancing in those days was nothing like it is now. Then it was good, clean fun, at least in our home it was. We never knew any other kind.

You can imagine how we children hated going to bed on those evenings. We meekly obeyed the command to go to our rooms, and then tiptoed back out on the upstairs landing, watching the fun through the wooden slats. Eventually someone would notice us and Mother would send us back to bed again.

When I graduated from high school I wanted to go to Nurses College but didn't see how that could happen. A woman's place was in the home. Literally. But Mother knew how badly I wanted to be a nurse and encouraged me every step of the way.

"Celia," she would tell me, "we're going to find a way for you to go. I always wanted to be a nurse too, but never got a chance. If you want to be a nurse, then you will be a nurse."

I appreciated mother's support, but how could I leave her with all the work? Even with two other sisters, I knew she would feel my absence and I didn't like to think of causing her any hardship. I finally came up with the only solution I could think of.

"Dad, you are going to have to get mother a washing machine," I told him one day. I had seen a picture of one in a catalogue that had come in the mail from Great Falls and realized that this was obviously the answer. "I need to go to nursing college, and the only way I can leave Mother, is if you will make it easier for her to get the work done without me."

That modern machine was my ticket to Great Falls and enroll in nursing college.

Dad agreed, and bought mother her first washing machine. We set it up in the basement and marveled at a technology that could figure out how to create a wringer to help the clothes dry faster after you hung them on the clothes line outside. That modern machine was my ticket to go to Great Falls and enroll in nursing college.

Even then, without my knowing it, God was preparing me for my future. I wanted to be a nurse so I could help people. But I had no way of knowing that this education was also preparing me for the medical emergencies we faced as a family while traveling around the world. When the kids got sick Daddy and I never ran to a doctor. First we prayed, and then I used the practical knowledge I learned as a young woman in that Montana nursing college. I knew not to panic when my son showed signs of having polio, or when Daddy got malaria in Africa, or when someone needed me to help deliver a baby. No matter where we lived, it seemed someone around me usually needed to be cared for and I often thanked God for my training.

I look back to those happy carefree days as a child on our farm and later as a young nurse and see God forming and shaping me even then when I wasn't aware of what He had in store for me.

Isn't it something to think that even as small children, God is looking after us, guiding our footsteps? The blueprint for all of our days was in His mind before we were born. Even when we are unaware of it, God is leading us into the plan He has for our lives. That's why you and I don't need to fret so much about our next move. God is already there ahead of time and has been preparing us for the next step on the journey. He never wastes any experience we have, good or bad.

"All the days ordained for me were written in your book before one of them came to be." (Psalm 139: 16)

CHAPTER FIVE

Wisdom Is...Telling the Old, Old Story

The first time I met Daddy was when I had finished nursing college and was living with a friend in Great Falls, Montana. I was working twenty-hour days at the hospital and making thirty-five dollars a week. It was not much money for the long hours of hard work and making ends meet was not easy. When a friend invited me to move in with her so we could share our expenses, I quickly agreed.

One day our iron broke and so she called a repairman to fix it. Today we would probably go down to Wal-Mart and get a new one, but back then we didn't replace things easily.

You guessed it. The repairman was John Dodge. I immediately knew two things about him. One, he was a handsome man with dark hair and olive skin, and two, he knew how to charm young women. Why else would I be flirting with this stranger ten minutes after I met him? When he unplugged the iron before working on it, I quipped, "At least we know he knows how to unplug the iron before he fixes it."

"Yeah," he replied. "I'm a smart man."

That harmless flirtation led to a date...and then another one.... and then another one. Neither one of us had any money, not even enough to go to a movie, so we just walked in the park and talked.

When we decided to get married we went to the Methodist church and had the preacher marry us. Just like that. My poor mother! I'm sure she would have liked for me to have a nice wedding with the community and family and friends I grew up with. But I knew there was no way mother was going to accept my choice in a husband.

As it turned out, I was right. She and John Dodge were like oil and water until the day she died. They were like two people who came from two different worlds and who both spoke a foreign language the other one could not understand. Mother was a traditional Norwegian Lutheran, and had lived in one place most of her life. John Dodge was an unorthodox adventurer and pioneer who never stayed in one place very long. There was nothing traditional about him. In fact, he came from a long line of settlers, pioneers, and visionaries and you could tell he had their blood in him.

His grandfather was the nephew of Stonewall Jackson, one of the great heroes of the Civil War. His father, John Roy Dodge, was credited with helping settle and develop North and South Dakota. His father and uncles were pioneers and doctors and businessmen who were well known in the Northwest for blazing new trails in the barren land of the plains. People called them the "honest Dodge boys." Besides being known for helping whole communities of people, they knew how to work hard and to endure the rough life of that time. Blizzards and dust storms, Indians and epidemics, they conquered them all with a stoic understanding that life wasn't about fun or necessarily being happy. You just did what you had to do. John Roy Dodge, Daddy's father, died in the terrible flu epidemic of 1918.

Blizzards and dust storms, Indians and epidemics, they conquered them all with a stoic understanding that life wasn't about fun or necessarily being happy.

I guess you'd have to watch an old black and white movie to understand Daddy's background. His roots were a lot like the old cowboy and Indian stories. In fact he tells about the time when Indians actually came to his father's house out on the prairie. It was during the time of much upheaval when the Sioux Indians were angry with the new homesteading settlers pouring into their area, taking land that had belonged to their forefathers. Those were the days

I soon learned

that he could no

more quit drinking

by himself than

he could change

the color of his skin.

when hostility between the white man and Indian often erupted into downright slaughter. John Roy Dodge, Daddy's father, welcomed the Indians onto his land and even gave them rifles to help them in hunting. It turned out to be a wise move. The next year the Indians came back to visit the Dodge family, offering their gifts of ponies as a sign of their friendship.

John Roy started drinking and the whole town watched while his life spun out of control. Alcoholism soon robbed him of his good name, shadowing his good deeds in the community with outrageous behavior that left him looking more like a fool than a hero. On one of his whiskey sprees, he hopped on his horse with his rifle, intending to shoot up the whole town. Instead, he shot his own horse right out from under himself. What a sight that must have been!

Without knowing it, John Roy handed down his alcoholism to his son John just as sure as he gave him his name. "Son, you are a worse alcoholic than your father ever was," Daddy's mother told him when he was a young man. And it was true. He had started hanging out in bars and pool halls, gambling away any earnings he had made during the week. He couldn't even keep a job for very long. Instead, he quit when he got tired or bored or knew he was going to get fired because of his drinking. His father had owned a hotel (Daddy started out as a bellhop), then moved on to working in a feed store and finally became a "profits clerk."

Though I didn't know it when I married him, Daddy had already become addicted to both alcohol and gambling in his early twenties. It didn't take me long to find out. The first time he stumbled home late and drunk I was shocked and dismayed. But he promised me it would never happen again, and of course I believed him. But I soon learned that he could no more quit drinking by himself than he could change the color of his skin.

Both of our lives would have been a lot different if it weren't for a friend

Daddy met about that time. His name was Ivan, a man who was handicapped with a severe limp when he walked, and yet it was obvious right from the start that he loved God deeply. Daddy and he became good friends and started spending a lot of time together.

"John, you need Jesus in your heart," Ivan told him. This was news to Daddy, but the Spirit of the Lord began to convict him and he started asking Ivan more questions about Jesus. The two of them would go off into the hills and walk and talk and pray for hours.

The burden of all the years of drinking, cheating, and brawling fell off of him in a moment's time.

One day, while walking home through a Montana public park, Daddy passed a pond with beautiful white swans swimming by.

"Your sins are as white as snow, just like the swans."

The words were strong in his heart, just as strong as if someone had spoken them out loud. No one had taught him that God speaks to listening hearts, but in that instant he knew that it was the voice of God. Daddy dropped to his knees, right there by the pond with the swans and people passing by. The burden of all the years of drinking, cheating, and brawling fell off of him in a moment's time. He began to weep and call out to God.

It was an unusual sight, a man weeping and praying in the public park.

"He's drunk," he heard someone say as they passed by.

"No, I don't think so. I think there's something in the Bible about this," another woman replied.

Daddy knew he was making a spectacle of himself but he didn't care what they thought. He had been drunk in the same park many times before, making a fool of himself and he hadn't cared what people thought then. Why should he care now? He had just heard the voice of God for the first time in his whole life and he wasn't going to let people's opinion stop him from responding.

I always admired that about Daddy. I have never known him to care too much about what people said about him as long as he knew he was in God's will. Many times through the years, family and friends thought he was crazy, but that never stopped him. The same boldness that caused him to kneel down and pray in public, is the same boldness that made him confident that we could go anywhere and do anything God told us to do.

> *The same boldness…*
>
> *made him confident*
>
> *that we could go*
>
> *anywhere and*
>
> *do anything God*
>
> *told us to do.*

When Daddy told me about what happened to him, I knew it was real. He started changing from that very day and quit drinking and hanging out at the bars. He had a harder time trying to quit smoking, though. He often bought a whole pack of cigarettes, smoked one, and then threw the rest away. A few hours later he would buy another pack, smoke one and throw them away again. I'm glad God finally delivered him because he was sure spending a lot of money on cigarettes. We found a church, The Christian Church, and began to attend the Sunday morning services. Daddy was baptized there and made a public commitment to Christ.

Later, when a friend told us about a job opening on the border between Wyoming and Montana, we moved to Sheridan, Wyoming. Daddy was hired to work at a weigh station for trucks crossing the state line. He and I would sit in the little booth together and check the trucks as they came through. It didn't pay very well, but we were happy to have a job. When we got off work at about 7 p.m., we'd go home and sit at our small wooden kitchen table and read the Bible until midnight. Both of us were hungry for the Word and wanted to know more. Since no one was around who could teach us, we decided to dig in the scriptures for ourselves. We copied large portions of scripture at a time, writing on into the night. I'm not sure why we wrote the scripture down. No one had instructed us to do this. We just knew it was precious and writing it again, after we read it, was a way of cherishing the Truth and putting it deep within our spirits.

Isn't that something to think how God put a little trio of mismatched people together? A nurse, an alcoholic, and a lame man. We all came together at the right time in our lives. I shudder to think what our life would have been like if Ivan had not obeyed God and told us about Jesus. But he did and God just took it from there. The seed of faith planted in our hearts took root. We in turn planted it in our eleven children who have gone around the world with the gospel. I've

I shudder to think what our life would have been like if Ivan had not obeyed God and told us about Jesus.

often wished I could introduce my children to Ivan and let him see how his simple witness of Jesus has changed so many lives in so many nations.

Have you ever thought of how powerful your testimony is? Just a simple story told in a simple way can transform the hardest of sinners. That's why I've never been ashamed to tell people at the store or in the airport or in a restaurant about Jesus. Who cares if people think you are foolish? I always think, what if you save one soul from hell by that simple witness?

Never underestimate the power of the seed of the gospel once it has been planted in someone's life. Not only can you change a person's life through sharing the gospel, you also impact their spouse, neighbors, co-workers, and children. Even their children's children. It all begins with telling a simple but profound story of your salvation. When you tell the story of your salvation, you are telling His story too. There's an old hymn that says it very well:

> *I love to tell the story of unseen things above,*
> *Of Jesus and His glory, of Jesus and his love,*
> *I love to tell the story because I know 'tis true,*
> *It satisfies my longing as nothing else can do.*
> *I love to tell the story. 'Twill be my theme in glory.*
> *To tell the old, old story of Jesus and His love.*
> *(A. Catherine Hankey, 1834-1911)*

"For the message of the cross is foolishness to those who are perishing, but to us who are being saved it is the power of God. ...Has not God made foolish the wisdom of this world? For since, in the wisdom of God, the world through wisdom did not know God, it pleased God through the foolishness of the message preached to save those who believe." (I Corinthians 1: 18, 21)

PART TWO

GAINING WISDOM
THROUGH RAISING OUR FAMILIES

CHAPTER SIX

Wisdom Is...Serving Our Families

Everywhere I go, people ask me how in the world I had eleven children. "One by one," I tell them.

They laugh, but it's true. I never thought I would have eleven children. We never stopped to ask ourselves if we would be able to raise them or if we would have enough money to feed them. I knew God would always take care of us somehow and He did.

I can't imagine not having my children...or just having five of them...or even eight. Every one of them is precious to me and all of them have made a difference in the Kingdom of God.

Early in our marriage, Daddy and I decided that we would trust God with the number of children He wanted us to have. Yes, I know. That sounds strange to most people today. And it's a good thing I love babies, because it seemed He wanted us to have a lot of them! Every time I got pregnant again, Daddy and I were happy that we were going to have another child. From the moment of their conception we began to pray over their lives, claiming God's blessing, and believing for a fruitful life of ministry. We knew we weren't just having babies for ourselves. We wanted the nations to be changed because of our children.

I always dreaded telling mother I was pregnant. Our whole lifestyle was shocking to her proper Norwegian upbringing and she could never understand why we traveled so much or had so many children. Sometimes I would wait until it was almost time to give birth to tell her another baby was on the way. I knew what her reaction would be.

"Mercy, mercy, mercy, " she would say. The words always sounded like a mournful plea, but I'm quite sure she wasn't praying. I understood the shocked disapproval in her voice and knew Mother was worried about me. No matter how often I tried to explain the call of God on our lives, she couldn't understand why Daddy and I would bring another child into the world when we didn't have a home of our own and traveled so much. How could I ever make her understand our life?

I had most of my babies at home. I always tried to have a midwife present, and Daddy was always there by my side, helping too. By the time the younger children were born he was trained and knew exactly what to do. In fact, a few times when the midwife didn't show up, he had to deliver his own child.

I remember when it was time for our second child to be born. We were living in the basement apartment of a church in Great Falls, Montana. I woke up that morning knowing it was time for this child to be born and was glad that we had already arranged for a midwife to deliver the baby. She was a parishioner in the church and when we questioned her experience, she assured us that she had delivered many babies.

"I know what to do. Now, don't you worry," she told me. And I didn't. When the pains started coming five minutes apart, we called to tell her it was time and to come quickly. I was never so relieved to see anyone when she walked in the door. She washed her hands and came over to the bed, watching me groan with pain. I looked up to see her face white with fear and knew we were in trouble.

"Now what do I do?" she asked.

"Move out of the way," my words were ice cold and impatient. I was disgusted that she had not told me the truth. It was obvious that she had never delivered a baby. I had to take charge quickly. This was only our second baby and Daddy looked a little scared too. It was a good thing I was a nurse, because we sure needed one. I had never delivered a baby on my own, but I knew what had to be done. Step by

It was a good thing I was a nurse, because we sure needed one.

step, Daddy followed my instructions and we both brought our first son, John Daniel Dodge, into the world together.

It never occurred to me to be afraid. I knew that childbirth is one of the natural experiences of life and I never expected anything to go wrong. Out of eleven children, only two were born in a hospital. All of them were healthy babies who came into the world without the aid of specialized prenatal care. We never heard of health care benefits at that time, but then we didn't have any hospital bills either.

When Daddy and I first started out in the ministry, no one taught us that family should come before ministry. Daddy had a pioneer's spirit, always ready to forge ahead into whatever or wherever he felt God was leading us. He seldom thought of how it would affect the children. He figured that if he followed the will of God then it would be a safe place for all of us. And of course that is true, but the problem was that we didn't always discern the will of God correctly. We also made many mistakes along the way. I suppose none of us parent perfectly and Daddy and I were no exceptions. Thank God that He has made all of those experiences, good and bad, work for our children's good.

Even without the balanced teaching on family in those early days of our ministry, I have always instinctively been a mother first. Whether it was on Tibetan trails or a church bench in the United States, my first concern has always been my children. Were they fed? Were they clean? Were they behaving well?

When we first started to travel and preach in different churches, sometimes the Pastor asked me to speak along with Daddy. Preaching was never as easy for me as it was for Daddy and I never spoke as often as he did. But I enjoyed speaking and I learned to be confident and bold in the pulpit, even though my personality is quiet.

I remember one time I had just started speaking and Juanita, my oldest child, was still a baby. I had spent hours preparing my sermon and praying that God would anoint me to bless the people. When it came time for me to preach, I knew I was ready. I stepped up boldly to the pulpit and began sharing what God had given me.

In the middle of my sermon, I heard Juanita crying and without thinking, I closed my Bible, walked down from the pulpit, and picked her up from Daddy's lap. It was a natural and strong automatic reflex. Fortunately for me, Daddy walked up to the pulpit, immediately opened the Bible and took up where I left off. He continued on my same subject without missing a beat.

I laugh now thinking about it. What must that poor pastor have thought? But I suppose it is a true picture of how I have always felt about being a mother. I love the work of God with all my heart, but I have always known where my first responsibilities lie...to be a good wife and a good mother.

Our family did everything together. From the time they were born, the children learned to love church and the ministry as we did, because that's where they were most of the time. If we had our way, every one of them would be a minister or missionary. I just can't think of a more rewarding, adventurous life than the one I have lived. But of course you can't make people, even your children, be something they don't feel inside. Nine out of eleven of them have been in the ministry, which makes me happy. But I'm most proud because all of them love God and are serving Him. That's what's important.

Now don't think that just because they are serving the Lord, that it was easy raising our little tribe. Just because Daddy and I loved God didn't make us exempt from the regular sorrows of life. One of my sons came through polio and another one survived a dreaded blood disease. We thought another one was dead for three years (but I'll get to that later) and I lost two of my precious grandchildren through drowning. There have been times of pain, conflict, tears, and times of battle when we learned to stand our ground against the enemy who wanted to destroy us. No, we haven't been exempt from trouble, sin, sickness, and disease, that's for sure.

But we're still standing together because of God's grace. In fact there are two songs I make my children sing every time we get together. When they were little they used to moan and say, "Momma, we don't feel like singing that right now." But I would make them sing anyway, because I wanted them to always remember how they will make it all the way to the end of this journey. Today they don't have to be coaxed. Each time we're together, we make up our own little choir with everyone adding their individual harmony:

> *His love has no limit*
> *His grace has no measure*
> *His power has no boundaries known unto man*
> *For out of His infinite, riches in Jesus*
> *He giveth, and giveth, and giveth again.*

I sometimes smile at the young women who are shocked that I have lived a long life of putting the needs of my husband and children above my own. They call it unhealthy. They tell me I should have been more assertive and put myself first more often. I haven't read all the books they have on this subject but for the life of me, I just can't imagine how putting yourself first could be healthy.

I am living in the future I used to look forward to when I was younger. I look at my children, grandchildren, and great grandchildren serving God and I know that all the sacrifices and hard work and weary nights were worth it. In fact, it's hard for me to imagine any other achievement in life could bring me as much joy as their lives do.

It all comes back to you, you know. I may have changed hundreds and hundreds of diapers and fixed thousands of meals. But now at ninety-two, my children take turns making sure I'm not alone and that I have everything that I need.

I remember one time when I was washing Dan's (my oldest son's) hair on the ship coming home from China. I had him propped up on the sink and was looking into his chubby, round face while I scrubbed his head when he said, "Momma, when I get big, I'm going to wash your hair." I laughed at the picture of my young son washing my waist-length hair. But times have changed and he's the stronger of us now. Now, ever so often when Dan visits me, he washes my hair and reminds me of the promise he made to me all those years ago.

I am a blessed woman. I have sons who watch over me, making sure I have what I need and daughters and daughters-in-law who cook and clean for me. I guess our roles have changed. That's why I tell young mothers today to not be discouraged or give up. Yes, it's hard. There are challenges and crises all the way to the end when you bring children into the world, but there are also great rewards.

Even after I'm gone, I will still keep having great grandchildren through my children. Those new children won't know me and I won't know them, but they will have a part of me in them. That just goes to show you that it's very important how we live and what we do, because there is another generation coming after us who is learning from us.

The Bible calls our children our seed and that's what they are. They keep growing and producing, even after we are gone. When you think about it, we not only live forever in Eternity; our lives, what we believe and who we are, keep living on through our children and their children.

"Blessed is the man who has his quiver full of them," Proverbs says about having children. I don't know how many can fit into a quiver but I figure eleven is a tight fit.

"Unless a grain of wheat falls into the ground and dies it remains alone, but if it dies it produces much grain," the Bible says in John 12:24. There are always opportunities for us to practice falling into the ground and putting our desires behind the needs of our families. It's funny how that works. You think you are dying at the time, but actually, it's the only way to keep living and to make sure those coming after you are grounded in good soil. I learned a long time ago, you can't just think of the present. You have to keep the future in mind with every choice you make. Investing in our children and husbands by serving their needs, is one of the ways we are fruitful in the kingdom of God.

"Here am I and the children whom the Lord has given me! We are for signs and wonders in Israel, from the Lord of hosts, who dwells in Mount Zion." (Isaiah 8: 18)

Chapter Seven

Wisdom is... Watching and Praying

I never left my children, not for a day, not for a week, unless God spoke clearly to me about it. Wherever we went, we went together as a family.

The exception was a trip I took to Canada for a convention. I knew without a doubt that I was supposed to be in that convention, but it was impossible for us to take ten children with us. The meetings were scheduled for a week and that was a long time for me to be away from my little ones.

After much prayer about the matter, I decided to go. A friend offered to take care of the children for me; so I took the baby, who was only a few months old, and left the rest with her for a week. (I can hear you asking, "Where did you find a friend who would take care of nine extra children?" I'll tell you more about her later.)

Every day at noon, I slipped away to the meeting hall to pray while everyone else was in the cafeteria for lunch. It seemed to be the only time I could find to get alone with God with so many people around. One day while praying through the lunch hour, I knew something was wrong at home. Don't ask me how I knew, I just knew. The Holy Spirit was alerting me to pray for my children.

I said, "Lord, there's something wrong at home. Now you know God that I came only to seek You. I didn't come here for pleasure. I came because I needed to seek your face. So, now Lord, please take care of my children. If anybody's sick Lord, I pray that You will heal them." I prayed for my children for at least an hour. I couldn't imagine what was wrong, but finally after much prayer, I felt a release in my spirit and knew that everything was all right.

"Lord," I prayed, "whatever was wrong, I believe You've taken care of it and I thank you." I felt perfect peace about the matter.

Now, I am sure you are wondering why I didn't just pick up the phone and call to check on my children. Well, I would today, but this was over fifty years ago. In those days, not everyone had a telephone. Telegrams were the way we communicated long distance and even then, we only used them to announce births or deaths or very important news. The conference grounds were outside the city and so there was no way to send or receive news.

When I got home a week later, I said, "Who was sick?"

"Nobody was sick," the children replied.

"Well, then, who got hurt?"

"Nobody got hurt," they insisted.

I thought, well, that's funny. If nobody got hurt and nobody was sick, why was I travailing in prayer for my children when nothing was wrong?

Two days later, one of the little kids said, "Momma, Juanita almost drowned."

"When?" I asked.

"When you were in Canada."

"What day did this happen?" I prodded some more.

"It was Tuesday at about noon. When she went under the water the third time, Mrs. Baldwin got there in time to get her out."

I don't believe it was a coincidence that I was praying while my daughter was drowning.

Now isn't that children for you? I had told them not to go swimming in the river by my friend's house while I was gone. I knew they loved to play in the water, but none of them were strong swimmers. Unless someone was watching them every minute while they were in the water, it was dangerous and I knew it.

Thank God for the Holy Spirit who alerted me to pray. When people ask me how I know God hears me when I pray, I tell them stories of answered prayer like that one. I don't believe it was a coincidence that I was praying while my daughter was drowning. I believe God turned to one of the angels assigned to take care of our children and said, "Little Angel, you just go down and take care of Celia's children. She's praying for her children and telling me that she wants to see My Face more than she wants anything else."

My little Juanita was spared that day. She's the oldest child and the one who has helped me take care of all the rest. What would I have ever done without her? What would I have done without the power of prayer?

The best protection plan of the universe is the Holy Spirit alerting us to pray for our loved ones. He alone can see the hidden danger all around us and urges us to be vigilant in prayer. It is His grace that alerts us to pray and it is the same grace that gives us the words to pray when we don't know how. Are we listening? Are we praying? Sometimes it is the difference between life and death.

"...For we do not know what we should pray for as we ought, but the Spirit Himself makes intercession for us with groanings which cannot be uttered. Now He who searches the heart knows what the mind of the Spirit is because He makes intercession for the saints according to the will of God." (Romans 8: 26, 27)

Chapter Eight

Wisdom Is...Building Faith Through Our Words

I learned a lot about faith through a mother and daughter I met in Spokane, Washington. It was during a time when Daddy and I lived in the basement of a church and spent our evenings ministering at two store-front-missions in downtown Spokane. One was on Main Street and the other one was on Third Street. When we finished at one mission we would run over to the other mission and start all over again. We prayed and preached and passed out tracts until late into the night. It was an exciting time in our ministry because we were seeing people get saved every night.

I was pregnant at the time and Dad and I knew it was going to be a girl. In fact, with each of our eleven children, we knew ahead of time what we were going to have, and had a name picked out. Well, except one. We thought Faith, our third daughter, was going to be a boy and had decided to call "him" Paul. She was quite a surprise! But then Paul did come. He was born two years after Faith. So I guess we just got our timing mixed up, that's all.

During my pregnancy, we met a mother and daughter who became our friends and told me they wanted to help deliver the child I was carrying. Both of them insisted that the basement we were living in was no place to have a baby, and invited me into their home. When I walked into their small white frame house, I could see that they had everything prepared for the birth. It was amazing how God kept bringing people like them into our lives to bless us and take care of us when we needed help.

This was my third child and the second time I was giving birth outside of a hospital. Even though I knew I would not have the aid of a doctor, God was with me and that was enough. I refused to be afraid. That is, until the mother prayed for me. She hovered over my bed during my labor and kept crying her prayers out to God in a tiny, high-pitched voice, "Ooooh God, please help poor Sister Dodge. Po-o-or Sister Dodge. O God please help her." Her presence was heavy and sad and I could feel the fear in her voice. It turned out to be contagious.

"Yes, God," I said to myself. "Please help po-o-o-o-r Sister Dodge." O Lord, what if something happens to me or the baby? What if I don't make it through this? Did Daddy and I hear your voice? Am I being presumptuous to think you will take care of me without a doctor? The labor pains were hard, but nothing compared to the fear that was tormenting my mind.

About that time, her daughter walked into the room, laid her hands on my forehead, and began to pray. It was entirely different. "Now Lord, I thank you that you are with Sister Dodge and that there is nothing to fear. Thank you that she is going to have a good delivery and for the healthy child that is coming. In Jesus Name, Amen."

Immediately I felt strong and sure. The baby was going to be alright, I was going to be alright. Hadn't God spoken to us that we were going to have a girl? Then why was I afraid that it wouldn't happen?

I knew right away which woman I wanted praying for me. The daughter's prayer created faith in me and I relaxed. Besides, she was right…the delivery went well and my second daughter, Naomi Ruth, arrived—a beautiful and healthy baby.

You can usually tell if you are praying in faith or praying in fear by listening to the words that come out of your mouth. It's important to recognize the difference, because one negates the other. Our words are powerful whether they are said in private or public, whether they are directed to God, or to someone else.

I have learned to practice praying boldly and confidently and to speak the word of faith into my prayers. Even if I feel fear, I don't need to voice it. What good does that do? Fear is the enemy of our faith.

"And whatever you ask in prayer believing you will receive."

(Matthew 21: 22)

Chapter Nine

Wisdom Is...Finding a Prayer Closet

Not long ago one of my granddaughters asked me, "Grandma, how did you find time to pray when you had so many children?"

"Well," I told her, "I just made time that's all." Finding time to pray wasn't a decision that I had to think about. I needed prayer to live. In fact, if you were to ask me what the one key to all life is, I would tell you: prayer. Prayer has kept me connected to the heart of God and is the one unfailing source of strength for my journey through life.

No matter what comes my way, good or bad, I have always carried everything to God in prayer. I pray for my friends, for my community to know the Lord Jesus, and of course for my family. When you have eleven children there is always something to pray about. Someone always needs prayer for the unexpected events that happen to all of us whether it's sickness, transition, or a tough spiritual battle.

I guard my time with God as the most important time of my day but this hasn't always been easy. I never had a dishwasher or clothes dryer while the children were small. I stayed up most nights past midnight getting the last of the ironing done or scrubbing the kitchen floor. It was the only time of day when the children did not need my full attention.

But no matter how late I stayed up, I woke up at 5:00 a.m. to pray. No, it was not always easy, but I knew I would never make it through the day with peace and tranquility unless first, I had my time alone with God. Deciding to pray every day was not as difficult as finding a place to be alone. For many years we lived in a twenty-foot trailer house that followed us everywhere we went and privacy was a luxury we didn't have. We literally had wall-to-wall children. Jesus spoke of entering our prayer closet to pray, but what if you didn't have a closet to pray in?

I needed a place that was warm on cold winter mornings, private enough that I would not be disturbed, and yet close enough that the children could find me if they needed me. *"Dear Lord, what should I do?"*

There was only one solution. If I couldn't pray in the house, I would have to pray in the car. It was a perfect prayer closet because it was secure, close by, and private. We always bought large cars because of our large family and because I'm a small woman, I could even kneel in the back seat!

Every morning I got up early and stepped out to my private prayer room and closed the door behind me. No one ever bothered me or walked in on me and I could be as loud or quiet as I wanted to be. Many times after a hard day, I would slip out after the children had gone to bed and cry out to the Lord. It turned out to be the perfect hiding place for me.

Many prayers were answered in that humble prayer room. I developed an intimacy with God in those cars that affected my whole life. It was my secret place where many battles were fought and won. Often when we hooked up our little home behind us and traveled down the road, I could still feel the presence of God lingering over our family in the car.

After I discovered my quiet place, I only had one request. Every time Daddy would shop for a new car I would remind him to please find one with plenty of room in the back seat.

When young, busy mothers tell me today that they can't pray because they don't have time or privacy, I tell them about my prayer room. I learned early in life, you don't need everything to be perfect in order to pray. When we make a decision to prepare a place and set a time to seek His face, He works along side of us to make it happen.

Sometimes after you have asked God for a solution to the busyness of your life, you have to be willing to do anything He tells you to do. It's important to follow through with your plan, even if it's a little inconvenient. After all, I wonder if Jesus always felt like getting up early while it was still dark to find a private place to pray. (Mark 1:35) He knew that private time alone with the Father was the source of His power and strength.

How much more for you and me?

"But you, when you pray, go into your room, and when you have shut your door, pray to your Father who is in the secret place; and your Father who sees in secret will reward you openly."

(Matthew 6:6)

CHAPTER TEN

Wisdom is...Praying over Everything

Early on in my life I learned that there is nothing too small to pray about. Some people seem to think that God doesn't like to be bothered with little things, but I have always believed that God is pleased when I pray. Have you ever heard of a time when God said, "Don't bother Me with that now?" I haven't.

I have always prayed about everything. I prayed when Daddy or my children were sick. I prayed over the financial miracles we needed just to survive. I prayed for the child that seemed to be drifting away from God. But I also learned early on to pray over the small miracles I needed every day. And instead of nagging Daddy with all my desires, I told them to God and let Him be the go-between.

One time in particular I wanted to go to California to see my oldest son, Dan, and his family. We had not visited them for several years and I was missing all of them.

"Daddy, let's go out to California and see Dan and Bonnie," I suggested to him one day. We didn't have any meetings lined up for awhile and it seemed like a good time to go.

"It's not a good time," was his reply. "I just don't feel like the Lord is leading us in that direction."

Well, what could I say when he said God wasn't leading? I knew better than to argue and try to get him to change his mind. I don't know if I mentioned it, but Daddy could be quite stubborn sometimes.

"Lord, I really want to see my son," I moaned out my complaint to God.

"If you would just speak to Daddy and change his mind, I would appreciate it. But You know I want to do Your will, so You decide what is best for us."

I left my request on the altar and kept quiet about the whole matter. I didn't even tell Daddy I was praying about a California trip.

A few days later, he came to me and announced that he had changed his mind and that we should get ready to go to California. I smiled and thanked God for answering my prayer.

I decided that this way of settling disagreements was a lot better than arguing about the matter. Many times the Holy Spirit convicted me to submit to Daddy's plans when I took these matters to prayer. When I obeyed God we had peace and harmony between us.

One time I even prayed to God about my kitchen cupboards. Daddy and I had decided to ask God for a bigger mobile home. With all of the children growing bigger, our little green trailer house was getting smaller by the day. Buying a new home, even a mobile one, was a big investment for us and we took our time making a decision until we found exactly what we wanted.

When I obeyed God we had peace and harmony between us.

We made our selection, bought our new home, and moved in. Even though it wasn't as nice as a few of the homes I had lived in, I was grateful and happy. That is, until I started cooking the evening meal. When I went to look for the flour to make the cornbread, I realized I couldn't reach the cupboards. I was too short! How was this going to work when I spent much of my day in the kitchen?

I was heartsick. "O Lord," I berated myself, "how could I have been so foolish? We have paid for this little home and it's too late to change my mind." What was Daddy going to say when I told him that this kitchen just wouldn't work for me? That night I went out to the car and laid out my problem before the Lord. At the time, those cupboards seemed like the biggest problem in the world to me.

"Lord what am I going to do about this?" I fretted. "I have made a terrible mistake."

The next morning Daddy walked into the kitchen and said, "Well, I'm going to have to go buy a stool for you to reach the cupboards." The answer was so simple I felt foolish. Imagine me being upset over the cupboards and spending all that time in prayer over something that was so easily taken care of.

But I believe God honors those kinds of prayers because they teach us how to take everything to God. I ran to the backseat of our car many times when much more was at stake than my being comfortable in my kitchen. There was the time when Amos, my sixth son decided not to go into ministry, even though he knew it was the will of God for his life. I laid him on the back seat altar and saw God turn him around. He now pastors a church in Washington D.C. And then there was Timothy, my youngest child, who was not expected to live because of a serious blood disease. I laid him on the same altar of prayer and he is alive and well and enjoying his grandchildren today.

Sometimes I would shout and sing my praise over answered prayers and at other times I would cry and sob because of a broken heart. There were also those moments when I waited quietly listening to the voice of God while He spoke to me of plans for our future. Through established prayer God often gently laid His finger on sin in my life, or told me to apologize to my husband or children. Prayer has sustained me all of my life.

When people refer to our life and ask me "how in the world did you do it?" I tell them about the back seat of our car and my early morning appointments with God. That time alone with God was the driving force of my life. Come to think of it, maybe those back seat prayers were symbols of the fact, that without prayer none of us will reach our God-ordained destinations.

We have to become like children, learning how to take every care to our Father. This is the only way that we will learn that He can be trusted. Jesus raised Lazarus from the dead but he also cared when the wine ran out at a wedding.

If we have learned how to trust God with the small matters of our life, we will find that our faith in Him to answer prayer is already established. When the large storms of life come (and they will) prayer will be the automatic refuge we run to for safety.

Prayer is always the right response.

"Do not be anxious about anything, but in everything, by prayer and petition, with thanksgiving, present your requests to God."

(Philippians 4: 6)

Chapter Eleven

Wisdom is... Working out Our Faith

When one of my children recently bought me an electric toothbrush, I had to laugh. Imagine needing help brushing your teeth! To tell you the truth, I haven't used it much. It seems to me that we may have gone a little overboard on all these gadgets that are supposed to make our life easier. Not all of them, of course. For instance, most people have an automatic washer and dryer and the Lord knows I'm thankful for mine. I have too many memories of rough, uneven washboards, to take them for granted. My only question is, where were they when I needed them the most?

I remember when I only had five children and it seemed I could never get rid of the mountain of dirty clothes that seemed to be a part of every day. No matter how often I washed, dirty clothes just kept multiplying. I often thought how nice it would be to have a wringer washing machine, but we didn't have the money and so I used my washboard. We seldom had money for extra luxuries. We were just grateful to be blessed with necessities.

One day my oldest son came to me and said, "Momma, I need a bicycle." John Daniel was ten years old and needed a way to get to school.

"Danny, we don't have the money," I told him.

"All right," he answered. "I'll get one on my own."

He was only ten years old at the time, but he went out and found a job the next day. Every morning he was up and out the door by 5 a.m., delivering newspapers. In the afternoon when he came in from school, he changed his clothes and went out again to sell more newspapers on the street corner and in the stores. That little boy made nine dollars a day, which to him seemed like a fortune. He put away money every week until he had enough to buy his own bicycle. I was so proud of him.

One day he came in while I was scrubbing towels on the washboard and said, "Momma, I'm going to buy you a washing machine." I smiled at him, knowing no ten-year-old boy could buy a washing machine. Why, they sold for $150.00 and if Daddy and I couldn't come up with the money, I knew he sure couldn't.

But you know, he did. He put back ten dollars a month and bought me my first wringer washing machine. Danny had discovered that you can have anything if you are willing to work hard. From that day to this he has never been without a job or money.

One day he came in while I was scrubbing towels on the washboard and said, "Momma, I'm going to buy you a washing machine."

All of our children learned the value of hard work and working as a team. As they got older, the girls learned that wash day meant a whole day of changing the water in rinse buckets, feeding the wringer wet, dripping clothes, and hanging them out to dry. Of course after they were dry they had to be taken in, folded and ironed. My boys learned how to wash dishes, mop floors, and take care of babies. There was always plenty of work for everyone.

There were many times when God miraculously provided for our family. But He was also glorified when we worked hard and taught our children how to work. When the offerings in the churches we spoke at were not enough to feed us all, Daddy would pack the kids in the car to go pick oranges or pull onions or sometimes, they even sold Bibles door to door. At the end of the day, everyone poured the money out on the kitchen table and Daddy would count it all together. None of the children were excited about that, especially when most of the money they earned had to go for groceries and gas. I always felt a little sorry for them when that happened. But without knowing it, they were learning that they never needed to be without if they were willing to work and share their resources.

In a large family there are always many needs and plenty of wants. Our children may have never had everything they wanted. But there was never a time in raising eleven children that our family went without what we needed.

God's promise to us is that He will supply our every need. When we realize that He accomplishes this in many different ways, we won't fret and worry trying to figure out how He will take care of us. If we are obeying Him, we can rest in the confidence that He will create His own solutions to our dilemmas.

Living by faith does not mean that we don't have to work hard. Nor does it mean that God gives us everything we want. Especially if our "wants" get in the way of what He is doing in our lives. God is a loving parent who is not only concerned with what we need now, but also with the character He is building in us through the tough times.

There are life-lessons in every difficult experience. While we are waiting to see how God is going to see us through, we can learn to watch for His creative power. One thing we know is that He always has a solution and most of the time it is right in front of us.

"He called out to them, "Friends haven't you any fish?""No," they answered. He said, "Throw your net on the right side of the boat and you will find some." When they did, they were unable to haul the net in because of the large number of fish." (John 21: 5, 6)

CHAPTER TWELVE

Wisdom is...Living Light

I learned one of the most valuable lessons of my life in Atlanta, Georgia. Daddy and I, along with five of the children, were living in a small green trailer house that we pulled behind us everywhere we went. Everything we owned in this world was in that twenty-foot-long house on wheels.

"How do you all fit in there?" people would ask in amazement when they saw where we lived. I had to admit that it was crowded, but it never bothered me. I had already learned how to be at home anywhere I laid my head to rest. Wherever God told us to go, that was my home. I didn't mind if it was small, or if we were crowded, but it had to be clean. Through the years I have lived in a cement building in Africa, a barn in Tibet, and one time, a granary in China. In Hawaii, we had a nice big house on the Pacific Ocean with a front yard of sand and clear blue water. And in Coeur d' Alene, Idaho, I lived in the back of a storefront where we pioneered a small church.

But when we started criss-crossing the States preaching revivals in churches from Texas to Montana, it just seemed more logical to pull our home behind us. It was not unusual to stop on our way to another church revival and spend the night by the side of the road before getting up before dawn to start out again. All of us learned to fall asleep to the sounds of huge eighteen-wheelers whizzing by, shaking our rubber-wheeled foundation in their rumbling wake. That never bothered me. As long as I had my children around me, I figured we were home. All of our children learned how to wake up to a new front yard every week or so, whether it was a church parking lot, a mobile home park, or the back of someone's large lawn. Their security was knowing that Daddy and I would always be there with them.

While we were in Atlanta we parked the mobile home near the large church where we were attending a conference for the week. One night after the evening service, we returned home to find that our clothes were strewn everywhere. Drawers and cupboards were left open, some of them turned upside down on the bed and the kitchen sink was covered with books and papers. Daddy and I stood inside the doorway in shocked dismay. Someone had broken in and rummaged through our belongings. But why? Why would anyone break into a little trailer house, I asked myself over and over. It just didn't make sense to me. It still doesn't. Whoever it was didn't find any money and the Lord knows we didn't have any silver, expensive appliances, or anything else that thieves usually wanted. We lived a very frugal life style with a focus on the bare necessities. We had a bed, dishes, and enough clothes to be clean and neat. Not exactly a robber's dream.

There was only one thing in that little trailer that I was concerned about and I walked straight to the cupboard to see if it was still there. A worn green shoebox full of pictures, certificates, and old passports were the only valuables I had in this life—the kind of things no one but the family would be interested in.

It was gone. I sat down on the bed and cried, moaning about how I would have rather given them a thousand dollars than that box.

"Momma, now don't be foolish," Daddy chided me. He didn't want to see me cry, but he was never any good at comforting me or anyone else. That just wasn't his nature.

"Those were just things. You have to let them go," his voice was stern.

His words made me mad. They may have been "just things" to him, but to me they were the most important treasures of my life apart from the people I loved. I didn't have jewelry or fine clothes and I never wanted them. My valuables were documents of our family's history.

It was a loss that left me feeling sad and despondent for days. "Lord!" I cried. "Haven't I given you enough? I've never demanded a nice home or a conventional life style. I've given you everything I know to give you. It seems I could keep just something for myself."

It may sound strange to you, but I actually had a harder time giving up those keepsakes than I did giving up my home to go to Tibet! All week long I struggled with my feelings over that stolen shoebox. For the first time in many years I felt angry for not being able to have anything permanent of my own.

The emphasis of the conference we were attending was world missions and laying down everything for the sake of the gospel. While other people were giving away their hard-earned money and others were preparing to offer their lives to live in Africa and India and Mexico for the sake of the gospel, I was struggling with giving God my green shoebox.

I had given God my life and my desires and my heart. But I had never surrendered my "things."

I finally wept my way to breakthrough. "Lord," I prayed. "You can have all those things. I don't understand why someone would take them, but I'm going to give them to you so I can have peace."

That prayer was one of the most important prayers I have ever prayed in my life. I had given God my life and my desires and my heart. But I had never surrendered my "things."

I may not have always liked it at the time, but living with Daddy taught me to live light and to never let things bog me down. If we started getting too much of anything he began to get uneasy. He would start giving everything away so we would always be ready to move when God spoke to us.

To most people it seemed like a radical way to live, but that was just who Daddy was. When he died, everything he personally owned fit in a small box. He didn't have much to leave his children except multiple worn out Bibles and books and personal keepsakes, small mementoes of his life. He had several suits, but only one good, expensive one and before he died he asked me to not bury him in it. "Don't waste it by burying me in it," he told me.

"Give it to someone who needs it."

I was proud of him because he left this world without owing debts, but still holding on to his true riches which were in heaven. Eleven of them were on earth and gathered around his bed during those last days, worshipping God and singing their father's favorite songs for him. The nurses in that small Texas hospital asked if they could open the door so they could listen. They kept telling me how lucky I was to have so many children who loved Daddy and me, and who loved God. Of course I already knew that. How do you compare that with a big beautiful mansion somewhere? I always knew we were both rich.

I think of young couples starting out in life who think they need nice homes and luxury cars to be happy. I wish I could tell them that in the end, having the nicest and the best is not important at all. Pining for more than what we have is a waste of contentment. And who knows, maybe it's the reason God can't send us where He would like us to go because we have to have too many things. Learning to live simply might hurt sometimes, but in the long run it's the best way.

> *Pining for more than what we have is a waste of contentment.*

Even now, my children are always ready to buy me whatever I want. But I don't know what good a new color of carpet is going to do me and I sure don't need a new house. I figure I still have a lot of things to do and places to go and I don't want to worry about keeping up with belongings that are going to be moth-eaten and old with time. I have taught my children that life can be full of adventure if we don't have to have everything. As my son Dan says now, "You can have anything but you can't have everything." He's right.

For me, I'm glad I chose the adventures over the "things." Now that I'm getting closer to the other side of eternity, most of my treasures are over there instead of here and that's the way I like it. That's where I will settle down and quit traveling and have time to arrange my mansion exactly how I want it.

Recently, on my birthday, my family and friends gave me lots of gifts which were wonderful to receive. But in the back of my mind I could still hear Daddy say, "Get rid of them, Momma. If you don't need them, they just bog you down."

I've discovered that we never get through with giving the Lord "things" because we keep collecting them. Right after we give something of value away, we go on to get the next thing that we think we need. God understands that we can become a slave to our belongings and that's why they have to constantly go on the altar if we want to serve Him with a whole heart.

When Jesus said we must leave all to be His disciples, He was trying to tell us about the danger of loving comfort and possessions more than people. The key to living a life of fulfillment is in being willing to be interrupted by God and ready for anything and that's much easier to do if your heart isn't tied to your possessions.

"Now godliness with contentment is great gain. For we brought nothing into this world and it is certain we can carry nothing out. And having food and clothing, with these we shall be content. But those who desire to be rich fall into temptation and a snare..." (1 Timothy 6: 6 – 9)

CHAPTER THIRTEEN

Wisdom is…Releasing Offenses

We were driving through Chico, California on our way to preach a revival for a church in Oregon when I realized that our seventh child was going to be born.

"Daddy, you've got to stop here and find a house because I am going to have this baby any minute," I told him. I never made many decisions for our family, but when it came to having babies Daddy never argued with me. He immediately pulled over, got out and asked a man in a grocery store where we could find a house to rent. The stranger led us to a small, three-bedroom frame house where we immediately signed a month's lease. I had never heard of anyone picking out a house as fast as we did that day. I'm sure God must have gone ahead of us and prepared the way.

During times like these, the whole family became a beehive of activity with Dad giving the orders. "You boys unpack the car. Nita, Naomi, clean that kitchen up, we've got to use it. Mom lay down. We're not ready yet."

All of the children knew better than to sit down if there was work to do. And the Lord knows there was plenty of it to do in that house. I had never seen anything so filthy in my whole life. How could I have a baby there?

The older children started scrubbing down walls and floors with Lysol soap until the whole house smelled like an operating room. The girls made sleeping pallets on the floor while Daddy went out to buy a big pot to boil water for the birth. Of course there was no furniture to move, just some suitcases to unpack. It may not have been a home, but it would have to do. My pains started coming, hard and fast and I knew this was it. Ready or not, our seventh child was on his way. Daddy and I felt sure that it was another boy and had already picked out his name: David Daniel Dodge.

I have learned that few things in life are perfect. Most of the time I had to make do with what we had and this birth was no exception. Here we were in a strange city, and in a house that was barely livable. I didn't know a soul in this community, much less a midwife. But by this time Daddy and I didn't even bother to ask ourselves if we were going to go to a hospital to have the baby. We had become experts at giving birth at home. I can tell you, we weren't nonchalant about it, but we weren't scared either.

Daddy knew what to do. He quickly started a process that by now was familiar to both of us. He sterilized everything—scissors, cloths and sheets—and kept plenty of water boiling in case we needed more clean towels. He didn't bat an eye when it came time to cut the umbilical cord, and even bathed the red, wrinkled bundle of boy afterwards. The rest of the kids were in a huddle outside the bedroom door, listening for the first cry that would tell them they could come in and see their newest brother.

That poor little boy was in excruciating pain night and day and we knew we would lose him unless God intervened.

From that moment on, David Daniel never gave me any trouble. He had an easy going personality all of his life and was easy to teach and eager to please. When David was about ten, there was a terrible outbreak of polio in our community, and somehow he contracted this terrible disease. We prayed fervently for his healing, but he kept getting worse. That poor little boy was in excruciating pain night and day and we knew we would lose him unless God intervened. Desperate, Daddy and I fasted and prayed for David's healing. We had done everything that we knew to do, but he wasn't getting any better so we began searching our hearts for hidden sins. We both asked ourselves if there was anything in our lives that would hinder God from answering our prayers.

One day Daddy said, "Mom, I'm calling Pastor Wilkins to come pray for David."

Now I knew that Daddy was very critical toward this minister who pastored a church in the northern community where we were living. I never did understand how it started, but I could see him become increasingly bitter and jealous of Pastor Wilkins' ministry. I knew better than to mention this. It would only cause friction between us and besides, I knew it was the Holy Spirit's job, not mine, to convict him. Obviously, that was happening.

Daddy went to the pastor's house and humbled himself, asked for forgiveness, and also asked the pastor if he would pray for David. Pastor Wilkins was very kind and agreed to come to our home and lay hands on our son, even after Daddy confessed the bitter feelings he had toward him. Just a few days after that reconciliatory prayer, David was miraculously healed.

I have seldom experienced such a graphic lesson of the power of forgiveness in our lives. Would David have died if Daddy had not confessed his bitterness? I don't know. I just know that it's wise to live with all of our accounts settled and up to date.

Harboring bitterness of any kind always poisons our spirits and eventually contaminates all those around us. Children, spouses, and friends are affected by our spirit and often take up the same offense against the person we have not forgiven.

The gravest danger of holding a bitter grudge is that it affects our relationship with God. In fact the Bible says that it puts a block in the way of answered prayer. It is far better to confess our sins quickly and to forgive another's sins against us just as quickly. It's the only way to keep our spirits pure and our prayers answered.

"... confess your trespasses to one another, and pray for one another, that you may be healed." (James 5: 16)

Chapter Fourteen

Wisdom is... Training Children, Trusting God

I know what it is like to grieve the death of a child. I actually attended the memorial service of my fourth son and mourned his death for three years before I discovered that he was alive.

The day that I received the news that his car had been found on a beach in Gulfport, Mississippi was the saddest day of my life. The Mississippi State Police informed us after careful investigation that they felt sure he had drowned. His Bible and car keys were left in the front seat of his car, just like he expected to return and drive home. I had no way of knowing that he had carefully placed them there, masterfully staging his own death.

This was the first tragedy in our family and I was broken hearted. I discovered that it doesn't matter how many children you have, when you lose one, it is as if they are the only one. I walked through my days with a hundred pound brick inside my heart that weighed me down with a grief that made it hard to breathe or even pray. I felt helpless to comfort his wife, Nora, who would now raise three small children on her own.

At night when everyone else was asleep, pictures of his childhood ran through my mind, and I remembered how sweet he was as a baby, a boy, and then as a young man. I remembered how God had miraculously healed him of polio when he was ten years old. When he was twenty-one, he contracted rheumatic fever which damaged his heart and made it necessary for him to undergo surgery. Again God brought him through. I always felt that God had great plans for him and that the enemy wanted to destroy his life. *So why had we survived those crises only for him to drown at such a young age?* I cried out my grief and questions to God.

Three years had passed when I received news that an old college friend had seen David in Montana. Well, I have to admit that made me angry. How could anyone be so rude to say such a terrible thing? I knew David would never leave his family. I refused to believe he could be alive, because that meant he didn't want to be with me or his wife and children. I knew my son too well. That was not possible.

"Mother, you have to accept whatever is," my oldest daughter Juanita urged me during that time. "I believe he's alive."

When I asked her how she could be so sure, she told me that the Holy Spirit had been impressing on her to pray for him for quite some time. I had lived by the power of the Spirit all of my life and knew He had never led us astray. If God through the Holy Spirit impressed my daughter to pray for her brother, then it meant he was alive.

> *If God through the Holy Spirit impressed my daughter to pray for her brother, then it meant he was alive.*

Juanita was right. The older boys went to Montana to check out the story, and sure enough, David was alive and living under a different name. My heart broke all over again. I didn't know what was worse…to think of him dead and with God and at peace…or living in sin and rebellion and away from his family. I kept thinking of him lost and alone. I cried for his wife and sweet children. It was a sad, confused situation.

Several months later, my son found his way back home. For the moment we didn't care about why he left us. The business at hand was to forgive him and accept him back into the fold. The whole family of children, in-laws, and grandchildren gathered together for a "Prodigal Son Ceremony" where we lined up and one by one, embraced him and told him that we forgave him.

That was the easy part. The hard part was watching my son deal with the guilt and shame of his choices. Every day he woke up to the pain he caused his wife Nora, and their three children. On top of that, there was no guarantee their marriage could survive the betrayal, nor the years of separation. Holding his head up in the small, close-knit community where everyone knew their neighbor was much harder than living in a city where people had little interest in anyone else's business.

But it was not only his neighbors who were stunned. His Christian friends were shocked. David had been a minister and missionary, serving one term in a remote area in Nigeria, Africa. Without telling anyone what he was going through, he had become discouraged and then depressed, and finally slipped away from his faith and God. Instead of telling us good-bye and living the life style his heart had fantasized about in front of us, he decided it would be easier if we never knew who he had become.

Now he was reaping the results and I could tell he was miserable and broken. Nora had cause to never trust him again. The marriage was broken, perhaps beyond repair, his ministry was over, and his reputation was gone.

Watching David during those days was like watching someone rebuild a home that had been destroyed by a great earthquake. Everything around him was broken and my heart was heavy and sad for him. He was on his knees, bowed low in humility, picking up pieces, and then seeing if they could fit together again.

He traveled up to Montana and made restitution with the law where he had lived and done business under an alias. His apologies were public when necessary. On one occasion, he publicly apologized in the church where his memorial service had taken place. He sought out anyone he could think of that needed to forgive him and wept out his own forgiveness for himself during the nights when his family was asleep.

Several years after David returned to his family, John Mark, their seventeen year old son and Daddy's namesake, drowned in the river near their ranch in the Texas Hill Country. I had delivered John Mark and watched him take his first breath in this world and then later, grow into a young man who loved God fervently. He was a boy with a gentle spirit who loved sports and who witnessed and passed out tracts everywhere he went. I mourned for all of us, but especially David and Nora who were going through the fire again.

The fact that John Mark died through the very method his father had used to fake his death was a double blow. Would David and Nora see this as the judgment of God? Would their marriage stand this much grief? Would they both become bitter at each other and the world? I was praying more than ever that God would cover them with grace and heal their hearts.

Because of God's grace, both David and Nora have endured those times of great pain and sorrow and are still together. David's ministry, Ministries of Mercy, has reached into jails, homes, and churches around the States with a message of forgiveness and mercy. When he teaches on forgiveness and releasing the offenses of others, people feel the compassion that flows from the brokenness he has experienced in life. He knows that forgiveness is the only way to survive the crises of life.

Those were hard times for all of us, but now in my old age, David gives me great joy. He has served Daddy and me both for many years, making sure we have what we need. Of all my children, I suppose I lean on David's strength the most. I just can't imagine what I would do without him. Satan wanted to snatch him from his wife and children and his family and to rob me of his comfort during these latter years of my life. But he didn't succeed.

The hardest thing we will ever do as parents is to watch our children make mistakes. The worst sorrow is knowing that no matter how much we love them, we will never be able to spare them from making wrong decisions. It is far better to grieve their choices out in prayer instead of judging them or trying to control their actions.

After we have taught our children the right way, the most powerful thing we can do during those painful times is to be quiet and pray. After all, God, our parent, watches while we make our mistakes and assures us that His love for us hasn't changed and never will. Our children need that same kind of love. God is big enough to straighten them out when they step outside of His will.

"Train up a child in the way he should go, and when he is old he will not depart from it." (Proverbs 22: 6)

CHAPTER FIFTEEN

Wisdom is...Refusing to Be Divided

I have often thanked God for David's wife, Nora, who stood strong and faithful through those hard years when she thought her husband was dead. When he returned to his family she withstood the embarrassment and shame of knowing he had left her and the children and still, she did not walk away. The fact that they are together, pastoring a church, and together enjoying their first grandchild years later is a testimony of her character and love for God and for David, too.

It's important that we pray for the mates of our children. Choosing a spouse is one of the most important decisions our children will ever make. God knows how to perfectly choose their mates and does a better job than we ever could because He knows them better than we do. In His wisdom He matches weaknesses to strengths, and knows the exact qualities they need in one another.

Whether or not they make the right decision can make all the difference in the world. Of course, we all want to think that our children are perfect. But you and I know they aren't. And their spouses sure know they're not perfect. It's a good thing God balances the faults and weaknesses of our children with the good qualities of their partner.

I have been blessed with daughters and sons that my own children brought into the family through marriage. I have eleven 'children-in-laws' and I think of them as God's gifts in my life. They stand with their mates through the tough times and endure temptation and heartache and disappointments and help guard their homes from evil.

That's why I am careful to treat them just like my own. After all these years, I honestly don't believe there is any difference in my love for them and my flesh and blood children.

Sometimes in families we scrape up against personality differences and if we're not careful, we let the little things divide us. In a world where there is so much friction and disunity, we have to guard against that spirit entering our families. I can't imagine the sorrow of mothers and daughters or sons and fathers who won't speak to each other or forgive each other. That is an open door through which all kinds of evil comes into our home. Only we can keep this from happening to us. It's like I tell my children often, even to this day:

> There's so much good in the worst of us
> And so much bad in the best of us
> That it ill behooves any of us
> To talk about the rest of us.

A good reason to love long and forgive quickly is because you never know when you will need that person to help see you through the tough times. Not one of us can make it on our own. We need each other, especially our own family.

Families who work to stay close together during the difficult storms of life make it for the long haul and are still together to celebrate the joyous times. And you can be sure they will come…you just have to wait for them.

"Why do you look at the speck in your brother's eye, but do not consider the plank in your own eye?" (Matthew 7: 3)

CHAPTER SIXTEEN

Wisdom is...Cherishing Our Friends

The hardest time of my entire life was not in China, Tibet, Mexico, or Africa, but right here in the United States. I felt as though I was up against a stone wall and couldn't see any way out. And there sure was no way through.

When we were forced to leave China, we spent three years in the islands of Hawaii, ministering to the many different Asian nationalities and American servicemen who lived on the islands. We planned to be ready to move back to China as soon as the war was over, but instead, found ourselves back home again—a large family, with no place to live. We had no home and no money and ten children to feed. Daddy was seriously ill and he couldn't minister in churches and he was not strong enough to get a job.

Daddy's sister, Laura, had just died of cancer and now he had all the symptoms of stomach cancer himself. He was in intense pain much of the time, couldn't eat, and was steadily losing weight. Many times we stayed up through the night, praying and asking God for his healing and relief from the excruciating pain in his stomach.

My days were divided between taking care of him, a new baby just a few months old, and nine other children. At night I fell into bed exhausted, praying and crying myself to sleep. My dreams were troubled, as if there were demons all around us trying to kill us. In fact, one morning I woke up rebuking demons. Now I know that not everyone believes in demons, but I've experienced enough of them in Africa and China to know they are real. I also know that the blood of Jesus is stronger than any demon from hell.

We were in a battle and I had never felt so alone in my life. Usually when we had to walk through hard times, Daddy and I would encourage each other. But now I was bearing his burdens and mine together. Both his body and his faith were too weak for me to lean on. I would have to stand alone and pray our family out of this pit we were in.

"Lord, I just need to get alone and seek your face," I cried out to God. I felt spiritually and emotionally depleted and knew that just like the woman in the Bible, I had to push through and touch Him. I felt if I could just find a place to lay down all of my burdens and seek the Lord without any distractions, He would hear and help us through this crisis. I wanted to fast and pray and be quiet until He told me what to do.

About that time, I heard of a conference in Canada where well-known Bible teachers would be ministering. The thought of spending a week in an atmosphere of listening to the Word and having time to pray and worship was like a dream. *Dear Lord, if only I could go!* But I knew that was impossible. How could I take ten children and a sick husband to Canada? And I surely couldn't leave them. I felt trapped and defeated.

I told my good friend, Iva Baldwin, how I was feeling because I knew she would understand. Iva had ten children of her own and knew plenty about bearing burdens and enduring hard times. She was the only woman I had ever met who had as many children as I did, and when we preached at their church she and I hit it off immediately. She and her husband lived in a small three-bedroom house along with their ten children, but every time we were in the area, she insisted that our family stay with her. There weren't too many brave people like Iva who would have a family of twelve stay with them, even for a few days. But she loved me.

"Sis," she said, (she always called me Sis) "That's easy. You just leave the children with me."

I laughed at her. "Iva, how could I leave ten children with you when you already have ten of your own? I can't even think of it, let alone talk about it."

I went back to prayer and poured out my heart to God again. "Lord, please show me what to do. I feel like I'm supposed to go to Canada and that

I will meet You there. But how can I get there? You must make a way."

When I asked Iva to help me pray that God would show me a solution she said, "Sis, you already have the answer. I'm going to take care of your children while you go to Canada. The older children can help take care of the younger ones and all of them can help do chores. We can do it, I know we can."

"...you already have the answer. I'm going to take care of your children ..."

As preposterous as it sounds to me even now, that's what we did. She had two sheds out in the back that we converted into bedrooms. We set up a large tent in the back yard for more sleeping space. The children thought it was a great adventure and they loved it. But poor Iva, can you imagine having twenty children to care for? And not to mention washday! The girls helped, but it literally took all day long to go through the tubs full of dirty clothes and sheets.

Iva made big pots of chili and stew to fill their stomachs and then put them all to bed at night on cots and blankets on the floor. Since the Baldwins lived outside the city, there was plenty of wide, open space for all those kids to play. The setting was like a mini-youth camp with even a stream nearby where they could go swimming.

When I told Daddy that Iva was going to take care of our children and we could go to Canada he said, "Well, that's good, but we don't have any gas or money to get there." He had a point. I was so worried about my children I hadn't thought of how we were going to afford the trip. So I went back to prayer and began seeking God again, "Lord, you have provided a wonderful miracle in Iva, but I still need another one. We don't have any money and we must buy gas and food to get there."

Within a few days a minister from one of the churches in the area came by the Baldwin's house to visit. We had ministered in his church before and he said he wanted to bless us with an offering. Do you know that his offering was the exact amount of money we needed for gas and expenses!

There was only one other problem that I had not mentioned to God. We didn't have a car. So I went back to prayer asking God for one more miracle. By this time I was full of faith, because I was confident that God was making the way for us to go to Canada. A few days later another friend, who heard that we were making plans to go to Canada but didn't have a car, offered to drive us in his own car. We were on our way!

Daddy and I hadn't even left our doorstep yet, but it had taken a series of miracles to get us even this far. I knew somehow, someway, we were going to make it. If God was moving like this on our behalf, then He still remembered who we were and where we lived.

No one has taught me more about love and sacrifice than Iva Baldwin. She died a few years ago, but before she left this world I made one last visit to Montana to see her. I wanted to thank her again for saving my life, because that's what she did for me. Through her love, God began to open up all kinds of miracles for my family and me. All through the years of my life I have been supported and loved and held up through my dear friends like Iva. They are family.

When God wants to give us a miracle, many times, He uses our friends. Sometimes they are His angels on earth, sent to encourage and bless us. Other times He speaks His wisdom through their words or heals our loneliness with their presence.

We can make a decision to never criticize them behind their back or do anything to weaken the cord between us. If we have allowed judgment and offense to separate us from our friends, then we have also isolated ourselves from God's gift to us. Who will He use when we need help? To live without friends is to live without blessings.

"Do not forsake your friend and the friend of your father,
And do not go to your brother's house when disaster strikes you—
Better a neighbor nearby than a brother far away." (Proverbs 27: 10)

Chapter Seventeen

Wisdom is...Finding the Secret Place

Daddy and I both were worried that he might not survive the trip to Canada. Neither one of us would talk about it, but both of us felt that he was dying. For months, he had been in terrible pain and couldn't eat. He was surviving on a diet of grape juice that he sipped throughout the day and was steadily losing strength and could hardly even walk. I knew he had given up hope and tried to encourage him. "Daddy, you must believe that God will heal you," I told him often.

"That's easy for you to say because you aren't the one suffering," he told me. I knew I couldn't answer him and was glad that both of us were going to be in an atmosphere of faith and worship. God knew we sure needed encouraging.

When we arrived at the campgrounds in Canada, Daddy slept in the men's dormitory while I stayed with the women. I knew he needed me by him, but I was secretly relieved to be alone to pray. I had to touch God for both of us. Every morning I got up early and prayed until time to go to the morning service. When everyone broke for lunch I went down to the church to fast and pray some more. We were in service all afternoon but as soon as there was a break, I would look for a place to be alone and pray.

Ministers taught on healing and deliverance and the Word was going deep within me, building up my faith. I listened to the sermons all day long and prayed that the messages would settle deep within my spirit. The singing and worship felt like we were in heaven with the most beautiful harmony flowing across the congregation like gentle waves of soothing, healing balm.

I learned something more than what was being taught from the pulpit. There are many battles in life that we aren't supposed to fight alone. We need to be connected with someone else's faith and drink from the waters of other believers' worship. Those meetings made all the difference in the world for me. Both Daddy and I were being filled with new faith and courage.

We need to be connected with someone else's faith and drink from the waters of other believers' worship.

One day while I was in deep, travailing prayer for Daddy, I felt the Holy Spirit tell me he was healed. I began to thank God—absolutely happy because I knew it was true.

"Daddy, you're not going to die but declare the works of the Lord," I quoted the Scripture that kept rolling over in my spirit. He didn't say anything, and I knew he thought I was just trying to encourage him.

After I talked to him I went back to prayer and the same impression came back stronger than ever. Daddy was healed. *How was I going to make him understand that God had spoken to me?*

"Lord, You are going to have to tell him," I prayed in frustration. "Please let Daddy know he's healed."

The day before we left to go back home to Idaho, Daddy and I were sitting in the evening service and he leaned over and whispered in my ear, "Mom, I believe I'm healed."

"I know it," I smiled.

From that moment on, he began to get better. Though it wasn't instantaneous, his healing was the miracle we needed to make it. Daddy and I sang and rejoiced all the way from Canada to Idaho. By the grace of God we were coming up out of the deep, dark hole we had been living in. Our faith was getting stronger and I no longer felt the panicky despair that I had known for weeks.

We were living on miracles: this trip to Canada, Iva, the special, unexpected offering, the friend who drove us to the meeting and now, Daddy's healing. The trip to Canada had proven to be God's wisdom.

There are times when troubles wash over us like the waves of the sea and our normal prayer times just aren't enough to get us to steady ground. That's when we must separate ourselves from the cares of life for a season, and get alone with Him. It is usually always a sacrifice and we seldom see how we can take the time…or use the money…or take off work…or leave the children. But if God is whispering our name and drawing us into a secret place with Him, it is because He wants to show us a part of Himself that will transform us forever.

"And when He had sent the multitudes away, He went up on the mountain by Himself to pray….But the boat was now in the middle of the sea, tossed by the waves, for the wind was contrary."

(Matthew 14: 23, 24)

Chapter Eighteen

Wisdom is...Pressing in for a Miracle

After Daddy was healed I felt like a hundred pound weight had been taken off of my shoulders. I even breathed easier. I had been so burdened over our family's desperate dilemma. Now that Daddy was healed I knew that God heard our prayers for help. But when it was time to make our way back home to Idaho, I began to feel heavy and worried again.

I woke up in the morning and went to sleep at night thinking about poor Iva taking care of twenty children. I knew she would be ready for us to move out into a place of our own when we returned, but we still didn't have any money. The closer we got to Idaho, the more concerned I became.

"Lord, we've got to have another miracle," I prayed. "There's no other way around this mountain."

Even though he had been healed, Daddy was still thin and gaunt looking from his sickness and I knew he needed to eat. It was up to me to keep fasting and praying until God supplied all of our needs. I knew by experience that great obstacles are often overcome through fervent, fasting prayer. I was determined not to give up and break my fast until God answered our most urgent needs.

"Momma, you are losing too much weight," Daddy told me one day while we were making the long drive back to Idaho. I could hear the concern in his voice, but I still refused to break my fast. He didn't argue the matter but when we passed through the next town he asked our friend who was driving to stop the car in front of a grocery store. Minutes later he came out with a double scooped strawberry ice cream cone and handed it to me. Well, I just couldn't resist my favorite flavor of ice cream. The fast was broken.

I didn't realize it then but I'm sure God was telling me to go ahead and celebrate because He had already answered every prayer.

I couldn't see any place in scripture where it said to ask your Dad for a hand out.

When we looked at the map and saw how close we were to my mom and dad's home in Big Sandy, Montana, we decided to stop and visit them. I have always loved our old home place. Besides all the wonderful memories of times with my family there, it was meaningful to me that my father built it. He took pride in his work and attended to every detail. In fact, it was the most beautiful home on the prairie while I was growing up. Today our original homestead is a part of the Heritage Society…still standing proud and beautiful years after Dad has gone.

Daddy and I hadn't had a home of our own for quite some time and being in my parent's home felt like a safe, peaceful haven. That night I went to bed refusing to worry about anything until it was time to leave and be on our way the next day.

Of course I wasn't going to mention any of our problems to Mother and Dad. They worried about us as it was. And it would only confirm to them that we didn't know what we were talking about when we told them that God would take care of us. Besides, I couldn't see any place in scripture where it said to ask your Dad for a hand out. So Daddy and I acted like we didn't have a care in the world while we were in their house.

The next morning, my Dad called me aside, "Celia, I want to talk to you."

I thought of all the times I had heard those words as a child. Much of the time it meant I had been mischievous and needed a good talking to. But today there was a lightness in his voice and he was smiling.

"I'm going to buy you a house. Where do you want it?"

"What did you say?" My heart was beating so loudly I wasn't sure I had heard right.

"I want you to have a home and I need to know where you want it."

When I tried to respond I couldn't speak. Imagine my Dad just deciding to buy us a home. I knew Dad wasn't emotional, but I couldn't stop the tears that were rolling down my face. It was too much to comprehend. My two Fathers—my heavenly one and my earthly one— were providing a home for me. I felt protected and cared for, like I had just been asked to come in from a raging storm and sit by a warm fireplace.

We told Dad that we wanted to live in Nampa, Idaho, and true to his word, he paid for our home there. We finally had enough space to spread out; the boys in the basement, the girls upstairs in the attic bedroom and enough land to have our own garden. We even had a cow. Because we traveled so much, the children didn't know what it was like to go to the same

If Dad was like that, then how much more must God delight in giving me the desires of my heart.

school all year…or have their own collie dogs or live in a neighborhood that was "theirs." It was a wonderful place of rest after our years of travel and evangelism. We only stayed there three years before we began making plans to go to Africa, but to this day, it is the one house the children think of as home.

For me, that home was always a reminder of my father and my Father's love. I never get tired of telling the story of how God delivered our family when we thought there was no way out of our problems. I learned much through that terrible time in my life. I learned how to trust God in the dark and how to press in and make the effort to touch Him for the miracles I needed.

I thought of how effortlessly and how happily my Dad had given us the new home, as if it brought him great joy to supply our need. "Where do you want it?" was his only question. If Dad was like that, then how much more must God delight in giving me the desires of my heart. It was a lesson I have never forgotten.

There are times in our lives when we must press through the crowd of problems that surround us on every side and touch the hem of His garment.

Faith will always refuse to give up. When we are desperate and don't see any other way out but through God, we learn a tenacity of spirit that pleases God. Endurance leans on God's strength to stand until the answer comes.

"The effectual, fervent prayer of a righteous man avails much."

(James 5: 16)

Chapter Nineteen

Wisdom Is...Being Color-Blind

Daddy and I never consciously taught our children not to judge people by the color of their skin, or the way they talked, or even by the way they dressed. We just never thought it was necessary to talk about those things because it never entered our minds that this could be a problem in their lives. My family came from Norway and Daddy was part American Indian. We lived in China, Tibet, and Africa, and several of our grandchildren have married Italian, Vietnamese, and Filipino mates. I don't see how any of us are more valuable than the others. We taught our children to love people regardless if they were rich or poor or white, yellow, brown, or black. How can we say we love the people of the world, send missionaries out to minister to them, and judge our neighbor to be inferior to us? I have never understood how that can be right.

We may have never *verbally* taught the children not to be prejudiced, but Daddy was a great example in teaching them to have strong convictions and to never back down on the things you know are right. He had a strong opinion on almost everything and he usually stated it whether you wanted him to or not. Of course this tended to get him in trouble at times. If he believed something, he would never apologize for following through on his convictions. On the other hand, if he knew he was wrong, he would usually humble himself and ask for forgiveness...if he didn't, I would apologize for him.

Perhaps the best object lesson my children ever received on standing up to prejudice was the time we were invited to pastor a church in El Paso, Texas. Now if there was one thing Daddy was not, it was a pastor. But those poor people in El Paso didn't know that…and until then, maybe we didn't know it either. It turned out to be a big mistake.

Everything was fine at the beginning. As the new pastor's family, we went door-to-door, sharing about Jesus and inviting people to go to church. On Sunday morning, we picked up those who didn't have a way to get there, loading them into our family station wagon. We always invited them to sit with our family near the front of the church so they would feel that they were among friends.

One of the families that started coming to our church was a black family with several children and as always, I invited them to sit on the front pews with my children and me. It never dawned on us that this would be a problem for that white, southern Pentecostal church. But it was. "We don't want to be integrated," the board told Daddy. "You will have to stop bringing that black family to church."

> *They might as well have told us to quit serving God as to try to tell Daddy that it was wrong to bring our new friends to church.*

We had never heard of such a thing. How could you love God and not love all of his children? And who ever heard of judging people because of the color of their skin? They might as well have told us to quit serving God as to try to tell Daddy that it was wrong to bring our new friends to church. He was determined to not give in. In fact, I think he started looking for more black people to invite, just to prove his point.

The next Sunday we went by to pick up our friends and walked down the middle aisle together just as if nothing had ever happened. I suppose that was our first family protest for the cause of civil rights. Not that we were thinking of anything so noble. We were simply walking out our convictions.

Those convictions walked us right out the door. When the church asked for Daddy's resignation, he was proud of one of the reasons why. No one would ever accuse our family of being bigoted.

Jesus is our example in everything. So when I see Him choosing a color He likes best, I'll choose the same. It just may not be white, you know.

Can you imagine how we break God's heart when we let pride or prejudice make our choices? Whoever heard of only loving people who look just like you...or think like you...or worship like you? How can God send us to the ends of the earth to proclaim His name if we see others as less valuable than ourselves?

"Judge not, lest you be judged" is God's warning to us. Our relationships on this side of heaven should be preparing us for the time when we are a small part of a multitude worshipping around the throne of God. They will be from every tribe and tongue, every nation, every color, worshipping God in perfect unity. On that day, we will all be proclaiming the same message. Without Jesus Christ we are all unworthy.

"There is neither Jew nor Greek, slave nor free, male nor female, for you are all one in Christ Jesus. If you belong to Christ, then you are Abraham's seed, and heirs according to the promise."

(Galatians 3: 28, 29)

PART THREE

GAINING WISDOM
THROUGH SIGNING UP FOR SERVICE

CHAPTER TWENTY

Wisdom is... Obeying Quickly

"We're going to China," Daddy made the announcement one morning at breakfast, right after his prayer time. I looked at him to see if he was joking, but in my heart I knew better. His voice was too confident. When he saw the look on my face, he repeated his message: "God told me we are going to China."

These days people go to China very easily, but in the late 1930's it meant a three-week trip by ocean liner that cost thousands of dollars. No one traveled that far for a few weeks like they do now. Once you made the commitment to go, there was no turning back.

Questions rooted in fear tormented my mind. How could we possibly raise the money required to get all of our family over there? And how were we going to have money for our daily needs once we arrived? What about the children? Where would we live? How would we communicate with the people? Who would send us? How would I tell my Mother and Father? What if I never saw them again? What if God was going to require me to lay down my life over there? Worse than that, what if I lost my children in a strange land.

I poured out my heart to God, crying and praying for His peace, but fear continued to rule my senses. I finally realized that the only way I was going to conquer this battle was to give everything to God and be willing to die in China if that would bring glory to His name. I thought of the words of a song Daddy and I often sang together:

Is your all on the altar of sacrifice laid?
Your heart does the spirit control?
You can only be blest and have peace and sweet rest
When you yield Him your body and soul.

(Elisha A. Hoffman 1830-1929)

I knew the Holy Spirit was speaking to me through that song. Before I could go to China in peace, I was going to have to lay everything on the altar; children, parents, finances, even my own life. "Yes, Lord," I prayed. "You can have all of me. Everything that is dear to me is yours."

I was amazed at God's grace that began to pour into my heart after I prayed that prayer. I stopped praying for peace because I was filled with the sense that God was in control. I began to even think different thoughts that were based in faith instead of fear.

...if Abraham could get up and go, not knowing where he was going, we could obey God in the same way...

If God wanted us to go to China, He would be responsible for taking care of all the details. Didn't He know the state of our finances before He called us? And He sure knew how many children we had. Did I think he was going to say, "O Celia, I'm so sorry, I made a mistake. I didn't know you had small children and I completely forgot about your parents?"

Looking back now, I realize that if I had refused to go because of all those fears, Daddy would not have gone either. We both could have said, "O Lord, not China. Could we go somewhere else instead?" But then we would have missed all the great adventures and miracles along the way.

Daddy always said that if we weren't willing to do the will of God when He first spoke to us, we would never do it. Now I don't know if that's true for everyone or not, but we believed we must be ready to obey quickly. We figured if Abraham could get up and go, not knowing where he was going, we could obey God in the same way he did. At least we knew where we were going.

Even though we had made our decision to go to China, we still had no idea what we would need, or how we would get there. We just knew we would go. The first thing we did was buy some suitcases. Our friends thought we were crazy and told us so. Many of them didn't think we knew what we were talking about. We were warned about diseases the children could get and the unstable political situation in that part of the world. Most of them asked the same question—"how are you going to come up with the thousands of dollars it will take to get there?" Our answer was always the same: "We don't know how God is going to do it, but we are going to China."

I never doubted we would go. Both Daddy and I began to tell everyone we knew that we were going to be missionaries. When we were invited to speak in churches, we asked them to pray for China and announced we were going. We even booked our passage on the ship…all in faith that God was going to provide the money for the tickets when it was time to pay for them.

We had firmly set our course. As it turned out, we didn't go for another three years. But we kept the vision and the word of God to our hearts before us, by living like we would leave the next day.

I found out that the secret of faith is to just keep doing the next thing we know to do. When a word from God comes into your heart you must act on it if you want to keep making progress. Obstacles and doubts and even fears begin to fall away when you take the next step. There is no use to fret and worry and wonder how it's all going to work out. Faith has a way of growing, once you make up your mind you are going to obey. Do the next thing, quickly.

"Then Jesus said to them, 'Follow Me, and I will make you become fishers of men.' They immediately left their nets and followed Him."

(Mark 1: 17, 18)

CHAPTER TWENTY-ONE

Wisdom is...Following the Leader

In January of 1939, we set sail for China on the Japanese ship, Kikawa Maru. The war in China had already started and it was a miracle that we were allowed visas. Obviously, our initial request had been rejected, but Daddy refused to receive it as the last word on the matter. He sent a letter back to the immigration officials, no doubt the strangest one they had ever received. He simply told them that he must go to China to share the gospel of Christ.

"China needs the gospel now more than ever," he argued with them.

Their reply came two weeks later. "As an accommodation act with the United States, China has agreed to grant you a visa..."

God had done it again! Whoever heard of the Chinese Immigration Department bowing to the gospel of Jesus Christ? The visa was not the only miracle. We didn't receive all the money we needed to buy our passage until the day before the ship sailed, but we never doubted that it would come in on time. And it did. We were on our way!

We were on a great adventure, taking life a step at a time. Who would have ever thought that the young, green couple from Montana would be sailing to worlds unknown? We had nothing going for us: no money, no degrees, and no powerful contacts in high places. We were holding on to faith alone.

When we arrived in Hong Kong, we contacted a missionary who lived there and who urged us to stay with him. "You can't travel inland without knowing the language," he advised us. "The train ride is a four day journey and you'll have to get off every night and find a place to stay. You don't even know how to order your food or ask for directions. You're not ready yet."

His counsel was wise, but we didn't feel God had told us to stop in Hong Kong, even if it was to learn the language before going inland. We had waited and prayed for three years before we knew it was time to go to China. We had seen God work in miraculous ways to provide every need. We sure weren't going to stop until we reached our destination. We believed that God had told us to go to Chung King, so that's where we were going.

When we saw the crush of people scrambling to get on the train to the inland, we realized that finding a seat for the long journey ahead would almost require a miracle. There were more people than there were seats and the passengers were pushing each other out of the way in a desperate effort to be able to sit down for the long ride. I couldn't imagine all of us standing up all day, but the chances of us finding a seat did not look good.

Daddy saw that the windows were open and quick as a flash started stuffing our children through them. "You sit there and don't move until Mommy and Daddy get in," he ordered them. Because of his quick thinking we all had a seat together which was no small miracle.

We had no sooner sat down when Daddy got up out of his seat again, holding the bag of tracts in the Chinese language that our new friend in Hong Kong had given us. He joined the jostling, pushing crowd in the aisles, handing out the gospel to his captive audience. Reading material was a welcome gift because of the long hours of travel ahead. No one refused his offer.

A few minutes later, a young Chinese man tapped him on his shoulder. Instead of speaking, he handed Daddy a hand-written note: "What does this mean?" the note read. You can imagine Daddy's excitement. This was our very first response to the gospel in China.

"Do you speak English?" Daddy asked him.

Instead of answering, the young man reached for his pen and paper and started writing again.

"I can understand English and read and write it, but I don't speak it."

Obviously he had not been around English speaking people enough to know how to pronounce the words he had learned in a book. Daddy immediately started explaining the gospel to him, based on the simple message of salvation in that tract. The children and I moved over to make room for our new friend to sit with us.

Daddy opened his Bible and began to show him passages that explained what it meant to be saved. One of the scriptures was from the book of John, "My Words they are Spirit and they are Life." I was praying quietly for both of them while they were studying the Bible. Finally Daddy prayed with our new friend who confessed Christ as his Lord. When they finished praying, he got out his pen and paper again and wrote.

When they finished praying, he got out his pen and paper again and wrote.

"I feel it. I feel it."

"I feel it. I feel it."

When we read his response Daddy and I laughed out loud for joy. He didn't know how to explain the experience of salvation, but we knew exactly what he was talking about.

Our faith was so strong at that moment, I think we could have walked on water. Not only had God confirmed that He was with us, He had given us our very first convert before we got to our destination. And without knowing it, we had led our own interpreter to the Lord. He stayed with us for the rest of the journey, helping us witness, buy food and find a place to sleep at night when the train stopped.

Eventually the time came for us to go our separate ways, but we kept in touch with him through letters. He eventually returned to his home in Vietnam and studied at an Assembly of God Bible School there. He wrote to us that he was going to preach the gospel to his own people.

Who can understand the ways of God? I've learned that when you are walking by faith, many times what looks foolish to other people, even Christians, is the will of God for you. That's why we have to stay focused on what God wants for our lives and not be so concerned with what people think of us. Even when we can't see the way clearly, He will guide us one step at a time. Maybe we make following the Spirit's guidance too difficult. When you think about it, it's simply obeying what you know the still, small voice is saying to you in your heart.

"I will bring the blind by a way they did not know; I will lead them in paths they have not known. I will make darkness light before them, and crooked places straight. These things I will do for them, and not forsake them." (Isaiah 42: 16)

CHAPTER TWENTY-TWO

Wisdom is…Guarding a Grateful Spirit

When we arrived in Chung King, the wartime capital of China, Japan had already started bombing the major cities on the coast and we knew it wouldn't be long before the war would find us. In fact, everyone was saying that when the weather cleared, Chung King would be the next to be bombed. In spite of this prediction, refugees were pouring into the city from the coast, filling up the rooming houses and every available shanty.

For three years we dreamed of being in China, but we discovered that the reality of living in a foreign land was much different than the exotic picture we had in our mind. We were among a people who couldn't understand English and whose language sounded strange and unintelligible to us. Open sewers and strange smelling foods frying in makeshift stalls along the side of the road were a shock to our senses. Our children gagged at the floating chicken heads on top of their soup and complained that people pointed and stared at them, often reaching out to touch their hair or face.

I reminded them that we were the strange ones, not the other way around. We were guests in someone else's land and had to quickly learn how to live according to their standards, not ours. Even if we didn't speak the language, we could learn how to let them know we were happy to be here in their country. We found out that big smiles and hand gestures went a long way toward understanding each other.

The biggest challenge facing us was to find a house. With so many refugees pouring into the city, there was simply no place to live. We had found a temporary solution in a small dark rooming house where the beds were divided by cloth curtains and where the bathrooms were chamber pots in the corner with another curtain hanging from the ceiling for privacy. Everyone emptied the pots into an open sewer flowing through the city and the stench was breathtaking—literally.

I went to bed at night thinking how far I had come from the sterile white hospital rooms in Montana where I had been trained as a nurse to fight germs. The gentle world of my childhood home with polished wood and shiny floors was a sea away. Thank God Mother couldn't see me now!

I could survive anything, I thought, if we could just find a little place of our own where the children and Daddy and I could nest. Somehow, someway, I knew God would move us in the right timing if I would just be patient. I cried out to Him in prayer every night right after I put the children to bed, pleading for relief from our cramped and dirty living conditions.

When I saw the huge room inside of the granary, I started looking for things to be thankful for.

"Give us some kind of home please, Lord," I prayed. I didn't even care if it was nice or not. I just wanted a clean, private place for our little family.

I knew God had answered those nightly prayers when one of our Chinese friends came to the rooming house one day and told us that she had found a place for us to live. "If you don't mind moving into a vacant granary, I think I have found your home," she told us. "It's just one big room, but there will be plenty of space for your family." I was so excited at the thought of moving out of the rooming house that I could have told her we would take it before we even saw it.

"Thank you, Lord," I breathed while we walked through crowded streets to see what she had found. "Whatever it is, Lord, I promise not to grumble."

When I saw the huge room inside of the granary, I started looking for things to be thankful for. The walls were blackened by soot from a hibachi style stove that stood in the middle of the room and I immediately thanked

God that we would be warm. The floors were cold, hard cement but I made myself remember all the dirt ones I had seen since coming to China. With a crawling baby, I was thankful that I wouldn't have to worry about insects. I could scrub the cement and whiten the black walls. This was a home that God had provided and we would be happy here. That dirty, cramped rooming house had served its purpose well. I laughed at God thinking how clever He was to make me grateful to live in a granary.

I laughed at God thinking how clever He was to make me grateful to live in a granary.

That night, Daddy and I lay side by side in one corner of the room, our children lined up on either side of us, both of us praising God for His provision in our lives. When any of us were tempted to complain, we reminded each other to think about the poor refugees who had lost everything in the bombing and had fled to the city for safety. Compared to where many of them were living, this big room was like a mansion.

Who said the will of God would always be easy? I was learning lessons about gratefulness that I would use for the rest of my life.

Gratefulness is a fruit of our faith that we must cultivate and grow if we are to enjoy the days we have on this earth. Like any other discipline in our life, we have to decide to be grateful, whether we feel like it or not.

Nothing will ever be perfect for us on this fallen planet, and we will always see reasons why we could complain. I've seen a complaining attitude break up a marriage and even a church because of the poison it spreads. Like a contagious virus, grumbling to each other spreads discontent with our children and friends but the greatest danger of an unthankful spirit is what it does to us. We take the chance of missing the great adventure of faith planned for us when we don't learn to adjust our attitude to gratitude. How can God send us where He needs us the most if we are complaining and whining all the way?

When we thank God for everything that comes our way, we can enjoy a deep contentment in God that makes every difficult circumstance in our life bearable. We actually share in the miracle of God's ability to change lives and circumstances through our attitude of gratefulness.

"In everything give thanks for this is the will of God in Christ Jesus concerning you." (I Thessalonians 5: 18)

Chapter Twenty-Three

Wisdom is...Developing A Quiet Spirit

One day we decided to go down to the ferry and cross the river to the other side of Chung King. We were only going over to the big open-air market to buy vegetables and household supplies, but the trip was an adventure for the children because of the rickshaw and ferry rides.

I dressed them neatly and talked to them about being polite to everyone we saw, even if they stared and laughed at us. (Whenever we went out with the whole family we stuck out like sore thumbs and knew ahead of time to brace ourselves for the constant commotion we caused.) Daddy hailed a rickshaw and after we piled in, he and the driver started a heated conversation. It seemed the young Chinese wanted more than the normal price for the ride to the ferry. Maybe we were too heavy, or maybe he saw that we were Americans and he could get more money from us. I don't know, but whatever the reason, he wanted more money and wasn't going to take us until he got his price. Neither was Daddy going to give in to his price.

"Get the children out," Daddy ordered.

"Why?" I asked.

"Because he wants too much money," was his firm reply. Obviously, he had made up his mind that he was not going to give in just because he was the American foreigner.

"O for goodness sakes," I grumbled to myself. "Don't tell me two stubborn men are going to ruin our little adventure today."

The children were disappointed and I felt sorry for them. After all, they had looked forward to this trip all morning. Why not give the man a little more money? But I knew better than to try to argue with Daddy once he had made up his mind. I could have told the rickshaw driver that it was useless to try to budge him. But I guess he found that out for himself.

"Alright," I answered Daddy meekly. At least I sounded meek. Inside I was still churning. I was angry with Daddy for being so stubborn, and disgusted with the driver who had tried to get more money from us. The morning had started out with light-heartedness and fun, but now the whole family was in a dark mood. The day was ruined.

We crawled out of the cart and waited for another rickshaw but the trip to the ferry was not to be. We walked back home, none of us saying a word. The children knew not to cry or whine and even though I was disappointed, I knew that was not the time to voice my frustration.

The next day, when we started to go down to the ferry again, the Chinese told us that it was no use, we might as well go back home.

"The ferry was bombed yesterday. Didn't you know that?" they asked.

For the bombers it was a strategic location because of the traffic going back and forth across the river. All those lined up waiting to get on the ferry were killed. In a matter of minutes, ten thousand people were dead. If our family had been at the ferry that day, we would have been killed, too. All of us immediately bowed in prayer to thank God for miraculously saving our lives.

If our family had been at the ferry that day, we would have been killed, too.

I had to silently repent for my spirit that chaffed at having my plans changed. I was so glad I didn't insist on having my own way and in the process lead my family to certain death. Few experiences have equaled that one in my life for reminding me to be silent and to hold my peace when friction crackles the air around me.

Developing a quiet spirit that is willing to give in to another's opinion or authority is not always easy. There are few harder things in life than learning not to insist on our own way. Even though we are sure we are right at times, God is often grooming us for Himself by teaching us how to submit in silence: to Him, to our spouse, to our boss, to our friend. Sometimes even when we think they are in the wrong, wisdom still says to be quiet. God uses anything and anyone He wants to, whenever He wants to, for His own reasons.

Even two stubborn men who can't agree on a rickshaw price.

"Do not let your adornment be merely outward—arranging your hair, wearing gold, or putting on fine apparel—rather let it be the hidden person of the heart, with the incorruptible beauty of a gentle and quiet spirit which is very precious in the sight of God." (I Peter 3: 3, 4)

Chapter Twenty-Four

Wisdom is...Surrendering Our Will

The good thing about living in a granary was that there was plenty of room to invite the Chinese over to our home. During the day we passed out tracts and witnessed, and at night we opened our home to anyone who wanted to study the Bible with us. We met a Christian woman who spoke English and was faithful to come every evening and interpret the Bible lessons into Chinese. We soon had nine young men coming every night who eventually accepted the Lord as their Savior.

When we taught them that water baptism was the next step in their walk of faith, they all quickly agreed that they wanted to be baptized. We found a small pond of water that drained off the rice fields near the granary. At the time, it seemed as good a place as any for a baptismal service. Later we found out the Chinese fertilized their rice fields with human dung and that little pond was really like an open sewer. I shuddered to think we had immersed them in that water!

Miraculously none of them became sick, and to tell you the truth, we were thanking God for protecting them. Imagine how awful it would have been if we had introduced them to Christ and then caused them to become ill by being baptized! I'm sure God purified that water ahead of time.

Those nine young men were fervent and faithful in their commitment to Christ. We could see their faith getting stronger every day. Daddy and I knew the time spent training them in the Bible would multiply and spread to others through their lives.

This was never more obvious than when the city was being bombed in nightly raids. Everyone had expected the attack and yet no one was prepared for the terrible confusion of a city in fear and turmoil. Every evening we saw people running everywhere, trying to get to their homes before nightfall, to find shelter. During those times the whole city shut down while families sat huddled in dark, quiet houses. No one knew if they would survive the attack or if this would turn out to be the night they would lose their home, a child, or a spouse. Fear settled like a dark blanket over the whole city.

Daddy and I had counted the cost of living in China during the war before we ever arrived and had a perfect peace, the kind that goes beyond understanding. We had already told God that He could have our lives if He wanted them. We also knew we were in the perfect will of God—the safest place on earth anyone can be.

At first, the Chinese thought we were crazy to not be afraid. One evening the bombing started before nightfall while we were eating dinner. Daddy wanted to see the bombers flying overhead, so he walked outside with his bowl of rice and chopsticks to watch while he kept eating. Our neighbors were horrified at the scene and thought we didn't understand the severity of what was happening. Later, however, several of them asked to hold our children. "If I'm holding your child I won't get hurt," they told us.

They were living in a city being bombed, surrounded by people who were frantic, despairing for their very lives, yet these young men had peace.

It dawned on us that we hadn't heard from our nine young men for a few days. We were concerned that they might be in trouble, so we set out to the factory where they lived. We passed blocks of houses shrouded in total darkness. We knew families were huddled together in desperate fear. When we got close to the factory, we could see the lights were on, making it an obvious target for the planes flying overhead. Inside, we were relieved to find our young disciples, well and safe, reading their Bibles.

"Why do you have your lights on?" we asked them. "Aren't you afraid?"

"We're not afraid," they replied. "We know that God is with us."

They were living in a city being bombed, surrounded by people who were frantic, despairing for their very lives, yet these young men had peace. It made you think of the Hebrew children surrounded by fire. We could see first-hand the results of their studying the Bible day after day, drinking in the truth of the gospel. While everyone else was hiding in the darkness they had found their refuge in the light of a strong faith in God's Word.

Those young new baby Christians had discovered a key in fighting fear that will work for you and me. In embracing Jesus as their Lord, they completely surrendered their lives to Christ, and in return felt His confidence, even in the face of death.

Most of us are tormented by fear when we are holding on to something too tightly. Sometimes it's our reputation or the way of life we're used to, or our children, our spouse, or even a close friend. I have found that giving up our life to the will of God in every situation sometimes means that we must pray until our carnal desires are brought under His Lordship.

God understands that we need His strength to let go of what our heart wants the most.

Once our desires and ambitions are laid on the altar, we can receive His peace in any situation. Those nine young men in China, knew that surrendering to the will of God is the key to strong faith.

> *"But what things were gain to me, these I have counted loss for Christ. Yet indeed I also count all things loss for the excellence of the knowledge of Christ Jesus my Lord for whom I have suffered the loss of all things, and count them as rubbish that I may gain Christ..." (Philippians 3: 7, 8)*

Chapter Twenty-Five

Wisdom is...Seeing the Invisible

Even though we were surrounded by desperate need in China, we could not get Tibet out of our minds...or hearts. We didn't know much about this small country between China and India except that it was a forbidden Himalayan fortress. It was very difficult for tourists to get visas into the country, much more so for missionaries. The Tibetan people were locked inside, unable to receive the good news of the gospel. We found ourselves praying more and more for them and their country. Surely there had to be a way we could go and share the gospel there. Everyone told us to forget about that idea. There was just no way to get into Tibet.

So why couldn't we get the Tibetan people out of our mind? We had no way of knowing that within a few short years China would invade Tibet and thousands of Tibetans would be killed (some estimates as high as 460,000 of them). Others died in prisons and labor camps. But God knew. He knew those poor people living on the "roof-top of the world" needed to hear His name. And how could they hear unless someone penetrated their fortress?

Night after night we prayed for God's direction and began discussing how we could get into that small country with the gospel. One of our interpreters told us of the caravans that traveled over the Himalayas and suggested that this back door might be one way to get into the country. As it turned out, it was the only way. Our missionary friend, Eugene Holder, and our two interpreters, Din-Dan and Hannah, offered to go with us. If God was laying this vision on their hearts, then it was for a purpose. We prayed together asking God to make a way for us to go. Everyone agreed that God was leading and we should step out by faith, believing that He would make the way clear.

And that's exactly what we did. A few weeks later we set out for Tibet, a small army of five adults and four children. We had no idea what we were in for. I had come a long way since starting out on that forty-foot highway in Montana and was getting used to walking into the unknown, but this trip was different. We would be on treacherous mountain trails that few foreigners had traveled. *The dangers were as strange to us as the journey would be: hypothermia from the cold, high altitudes, deadly rock and snow slides, and of course, the robbers.* We had heard stories of how they ambushed the caravans, sometimes killing or leaving their victims beaten and left for dead. Everyone who traveled the route we were on lived in dread of the robbers. As foreigners we would be more at risk than they were. We didn't know the guide and yet we were putting our lives and the lives of our children in his hands.

When it came time to start the journey my stomach was bulging with our fifth child. I balanced him in front of me with my two-and-a-half-year-old daughter, Faith, strapped to my back. Daddy made sure I got the most gentle of the mules in the caravan, but I still didn't know how I was going to make it up and down those steep Himalayan Mountains.

My mother's heart was weighed down, heavy with fear for my children. They were still small and seemed so fragile compared to the tall mountain range we were on. *How could they survive the cold, long days ahead?* I knew none of them were used to riding horses, and yet we had to maneuver sharp turns, some with steep inclines.

Naomi, my second daughter, was riding with her Daddy and Danny, her older brother, was right in front of them. Danny rode up at the front of the caravan with our Tibetan guide, holding on tightly with one hand and eating boiled peanuts with the other. For a four-year-old boy, this was a great adventure. He was completely oblivious to any dangers associated with our journey.

It was six-year-old Juanita that I worried the most about. For one thing, she was on her own donkey. *How could she hold on? What if she fell off?* The trails were steep with drop-offs on each side. If robbers should attack us, we would all be endangered, but she would be the most vulnerable. Because we rode in a single line, it was impossible to see her all the time. I couldn't even talk with her while we were riding because of the distance between us.

One day we spent most of the day going downhill. The mules knew how to maneuver the trails but it was still a bumpy, dangerous ride. Bump… bump…bump…over loose rock and narrow trails. We sat on wooden packsaddles with blankets over them and I knew that eight hours of this kind of ride could cause me to miscarry my unborn child.

"Lord!" I cried out in fear. "What have we done, taking these small children over these enormous mountains? What about my little Juanita?"

"Don't I have an angel watching over her?"

The voice was unmistakable. The message was the opposite of the fear I was gripped with just seconds earlier. I knew that God was near. His words were so tender, I cried right there riding on my mule. I knew I had been comforted but also gently rebuked and immediately felt shame for doubting.

"Why yes, Lord," I replied. "Your angel is watching over her."

Just because we can't see the angels of God doesn't mean that they do not surround us. According to scripture, God dispatches His special agents on our behalf to watch over us and protect us in all of our ways. If God opened our spiritual eyes to see these ministering angels, we would never be afraid. Learning to entrust ourselves and our loved ones into these capable, strong hands is a spiritual discipline in our walk of faith.

Faith is seeing into that spiritual world of ministering angels without the aid of anything except the Word of God.

"*For He shall give His angels charge over you, to keep you in all your ways. In their hands they shall bear you up, lest you dash your foot against a stone." (Psalm 91: 11, 12)*

Chapter Twenty-Six

Wisdom Is...Refusing to Take Short-Cuts

On our way to Tibet we rode our donkeys up steep mountain trails that wound around thick brush and clear mountain streams. Those mountain passes were beautiful but marred by the fact that thieves hung out on these trails, waiting for unsuspecting victims who were tired and isolated, far away from any help. We had four children with us and I knew at any time they could be hurt or kidnapped if God didn't protect us. We were at the mercy of any thief who ordered us to stop.

I fought fear through prayer. Every time a fearful thought came to mind, I prayed instead of letting myself dwell on it. I prayed in the morning when I got up and I prayed when I went to bed at night. I prayed for the children and for their safety. I knew faith was overcoming fear when I could imagine the angels all around us, following God's orders to stay with us and protect us from danger.

They must have been, because during our whole time in Tibet, we were never robbed, not on those mountain trails nor anywhere else. To the Chinese who warned us often that this could happen, it was a miracle. Americans were a rare sight in Tibet and more susceptible to getting robbed than the Tibetans and Chinese. I knew God was with us. Those steep, isolated, dangerous trails became as safe to us as my Dad's living room back in Montana. I discovered all over again that the will of God is the safest place in all the world.

One day, we had gone as far and as high on those dangerous mountain trails as we could go with our lone Tibetan guide. We knew we needed to join a larger caravan to maneuver the increased dangers of the high mountain passes. The air was thinner and we had a hard time breathing, especially if we walked very far. A few caravans had come by, but Daddy had to ration our money and when they asked for too much, he refused to go.

"We've just got to wait it out," Daddy told me. "We might as well make ourselves as comfortable as we can."

My heart sank.

The only place to stay was a small little shelter on the side of the mountain made out of dried cow dung. *How could I live in such a filthy place?* I tried not to grumble, but my spirit was churning inside. We couldn't go back, and we couldn't go forward. We were isolated and had to depend on the next caravan coming by, and the Lord only knew when that would be.

We cooked our meals and kept warm by an open fire made from dried cow dung and watched the smoke swirl up to the hole on the top of the roof, blackening the whole house in the process. We had lived in some pretty poor places since setting out on our life of faith but I had never, in my entire life, lived in such miserable conditions as that cow-dung cabin. I couldn't imagine a night, let alone a week in that place.

Day after day we waited for an opportunity to go, but there was no caravan in sight. The days turned into weeks and both Daddy and I began to fret. How long would this last?

"Why, God?" I cried out my frustration. "Why do we have to stay here day after day in this terrible, filthy place?"

"Patience, patience, patience," was all I could hear God say.

We waited for one whole month up on that mountain. When a caravan finally came by, we didn't care how much it cost; we quickly got our few things together and set out on the trails again. I don't remember when we had been happier in a long time.

A few days into our journey, the line of horses and mules slowed down and finally stopped. It was the middle of the day, too early to break for camp. We all knew our guide was too strict to stop for anyone unless it was a scheduled stop.

What was going on?

The whole caravan started moving at a snail's pace with a deathly quiet settling over the whole group. I knew something was wrong and strained forward in my saddle until I could finally see why we had stopped. A group of horses with dead men still in their saddles were standing in the snow, blocking the passage of our caravan. They looked like ice sculptures, carved for a museum. I had never seen anything like it in my life. The guide said they had no doubt been blinded in a snowstorm and couldn't get to safety in time. The snow and ice and fierce mountain winds had killed them. Their bodies were frozen into ice statues. Even the dog that was riding with them was standing up-right, iced in perfect preservation.

It was an eerie picture of what happens on top of those high mountain peaks where nature rules her domain, sometimes without mercy. Chill bumps went down my back when I realized why God had us wait in that filthy cabin for one month. He knew there was a blizzard appointed for the mountain ahead of us and we would have all died in it—Daddy, myself, our four children and the baby in my womb. I praised God for His gracious provision for us—a filthy cow-dung cabin on the side of a Tibetan mountain.

Many times when I am tempted to be impatient because things aren't happening as fast as I want, I think of those frozen men on their frozen horses. God always knows something we don't know, and that's why He asks us to trust Him. I've learned that often when my prayers are put on hold, it's because He's working in someone's heart or life (many times my own!) and He needs time to fulfill His purposes. None of us like to wait that process out.

Wouldn't it be nice if patience were given to us like a gift? Of course I don't rule out the fact that God can do anything for us at any time. But most of us have to develop this character trait in our lives through trusting God when we feel like we are living in a dung heap and can't see over the next mountain. Those are the times when our human nature squirms and squeals with pain through the uncomfortable process of not moving. Giving God time to complete His work in our life when interruption and delays seem more like punishment than provision, are the times when we learn the most about who God is.

We discover that those are the times when He is actually displaying His love the most for us.

"Rest in the Lord and wait patiently for Him." (Psalm 37: 7)

Chapter Twenty-Seven

Wisdom Is...Asking for Grace

The Tibetan mountains were freezing cold and it seemed we could never get warm enough, but I quickly learned that when you are traveling in a caravan you can't stop just because you are uncomfortable. It didn't matter if we were hungry or freezing, we learned to wait until the guide stopped for a break. He knew the danger areas, what mountain pass we needed to cross before dark, and the best place to stop and eat; usually by pure, cold mountain streams where we could all replenish our water supply.

Sometimes when we stopped to rest, I quickly washed some of my two-year-old's diapers in the near-by stream. I soon discovered that water that looked so clear and beautiful was also freezing cold. For hours afterwards, I rode with red, numb hands and arms that ached all the way to my elbows.

All of us were ready for the end of the day when we stopped to make camp for the night. Daddy gathered kindling with oil based sap and made a nice warm, roaring fire that felt like heaven on earth after a long day of riding. We made our beds on top of the ground and cuddled up as close to the heat as we could, while Daddy and the guide took turns staying up all night to keep the fire burning. When we woke up in the morning we boiled water and made a delicious butter tea. I don't remember anything tasting as good as hot butter tea on those early, cold mornings.

Food was rationed and limited and I felt myself losing weight. And sometimes, by the time I made sure all the children got their portion, it was too late for me to eat. The food was packed up and put in saddlebags and I knew better than to ask for everyone to wait for me. I berated myself for being so slow, but you know, I'm ninety-two and I'm still the last one at the table. Maybe some things just never change.

"Daddy, I just can't ride today," I told him. "What am I going to do? I'm too sick."

I knew I couldn't afford to lose too much weight while I was pregnant, but I was more concerned for my two-year-old who wasn't eating much either. I knew the journey over the mountains would take three weeks and prayed every day we would make it all the way to the end.

One morning I woke up from a night of sleeping on the ground, my joints stiff and sore. I was nauseated and faint and knew I could not get up on the mule, much less ride him for one more long day. *If I feel this bad in the morning, what am I going to do by the end of the day? I just can't do it.* "Daddy, I just can't ride today," I told him. "What am I going to do? I'm too sick." He said, "Well, there's nothing we can do about it. The caravan goes on. You go with it, or get left behind…there's no other choices. They won't stop for anyone."

I knew he was right. There was nothing else to do, so I prayed. "Lord, I need grace. I need grace today, right now. I want to lay right here on the ground and not get up. Please help me. Grace, Lord, grace…"

And you know, I got up on that old mule by the grace of God. That day was different from any other day I rode. The longer we rode, the stronger I felt. I began to sing and worship God because I knew I was experiencing God's grace. I sensed God's presence and strength with me all day long. When we came to the end of the day, I realized that I had felt better on that day than on the whole trip.

I learned that God's grace is always available, in every situation in life. The key is to not lie down and give up, but to ask for His strength and endurance. Every bit of my life has been because of God's strength and grace. I have had to depend on Him for everything, every day. There has never been any other way for me.

When you think about it, all of life is a long caravan ride. We move through our days with other people and can't stop just because we are tired and weary of the journey. There are children to feed, bosses to please, and relationships that need constant care. We have to take care of our homes, make a living, and care for our parents. And none of us have easy paths on this journey. There are steep mountain passes that we have to climb, dangerous curves to maneuver and dangerous drop-offs to avoid. It's not easy. It is never easy. The Lord knows many times we want to lie down and die.

God always has enough grace for every situation. And He says He gives grace to the humble. We have to be humble enough to ask and then to obey, whether we feel like it or not. It's impossible to finish the journey without grace, and fortunately there is plenty for all of us. All we have to do is ask.

"…My grace is sufficient for you, for My strength is made perfect in weakness." (II Corinthians 12: 9)

Chapter Twenty-Eight

Wisdom is...Investing in Individuals

When we finally arrived in Tibet, we had to start all over again. We were in a strange land again with no place to stay and trying to communicate with a people we didn't understand. If we thought China was hard, it was nothing compared to Tibet. The living conditions were much harsher and more primitive.

We found an old vacated building, large and spacious, that the Tibetans called a castle. That was stretching it quite a bit, I thought. It was a plain wooden structure built over a livestock pen, forcing us to live with the sounds and smells of pigs and goats.

In spite of the animals below, I was especially glad we had wooden floors instead of dirt ones which always housed scorpions and cockroaches. It turned out to be the lesser of two evils, because we soon discovered our new house was full of ticks and fleas. They were everywhere. We woke up in the middle of the night with bites all over us and scratched ourselves raw during the day. I washed the walls, the floor, and all the clothes with hot lye soap and water, but still we had no relief. It was no use. As long as the animals lived underneath us, ticks and fleas were going to be a way of life.

Nevertheless it was shelter, a roof over our heads. I decided to be grateful and settle in the best I could with what we had. The children were following my lead and I knew they would have the same attitude as I did. If I was happy and grateful they would see this as a great adventure of serving God. On the other hand, if I grumbled and complained about our conditions, I knew it wouldn't be long before they would too.

There was plenty to be grateful for. We were living on the top of the world where the air was crisp and clean and the water pure. Fresh vegetables and meat were plentiful in the town's open market and the hot butter tea the Tibetans drank, warmed and filled our stomachs. Sometimes the butter was a little too old for my liking, but it was nourishment and we needed it. Barley was plentiful and very healthy and we learned how to roll it and dip it in the tea for a satisfying meal. It's amazing how hunger can help you adapt your eating habits!

"I know you have wine because I had a dream that we were drinking from small glasses of wine and eating bread together."

I made up my mind to settle in as much as I possibly could to this new land. When Daddy bought me a Tibetan dress at the local market, I wore it whenever I went out. Even though we couldn't speak the language, it connected me with the people immediately. They laughed and clapped their hands and smiled when they saw me and I laughed and smiled back at them. We were the only foreigners most of them had ever seen and it was great entertainment for them just to see us and be around us.

Our first convert was a poor woman who was addicted to opium. There were many opium addicts in the area, but it seemed the whole town knew about this lady. She had no family and spent her days wandering the streets, begging for handouts to support her habit. It was obvious that she was old and frail, her body wasted away from years of using the drug. I knew she was seriously ill by looking at her. We took her into our home, feeding her, praying for her, trying to build up her body and her faith.

One day she asked us about the little glasses of wine and bread we had. Thinking her addictions were tormenting her again, I told her that we didn't have any wine.

"Yes," she insisted. "I know you have wine because I had a dream that we were drinking from small glasses of wine and eating bread together."

Daddy and I were amazed. She was describing the Lord's communion.

We sat down and explained the Lord's Supper to her, teaching her about the power in the blood of Jesus for salvation and healing and deliverance. We couldn't find any grape juice, but used some buttered tea and rolled up barley as bread. It may have looked like a strange communion, but we knew the Lord would accept our remembrance of Him.

Her body became stronger and even though she was still sickly, she was well enough to go back to her home. She was like an evangelist, telling everyone who would listen about Jesus and the power of the blood of Jesus. She was a strong witness for the Lord in that community because everyone in the town could see the changes in her life. Later she became sick and died and because she had no family to take care of her body, we buried her.

"She looks as peaceful as an angel," Daddy remarked at the simple graveside service we held for her. I was happy she was with Jesus and that her days of poverty and pain were finally over. I realized that if we never won one more soul to the Lord in Tibet, those steep dangerous mountain trails we crossed to get to this one woman, were worth the trouble. That Tibetan woman taught me to always remember that eternity is forever and that one soul saved from the torments of hell is worth any sacrifice we make in this world.

Even though there are multitudes that need Jesus Christ, we must never forget that we are called to individuals. Serving one person who needs you may not be impressive to anyone else but God, but you can be sure that He sees your hard work and has love for the one thing that moves His heart the most: individual people.

"...Come you blessed of my Father, inherit the kingdom prepared for you from the foundation of the world; for I was hungry and you gave Me food, I was thirsty and you gave Me drink; I was a stranger and you took Me in; I was naked and you clothed Me; I was sick and you visited Me; I was in prison and you came to Me."

(Matthew 25: 34 – 36)

CHAPTER TWENTY-NINE

Wisdom is...Abiding in the Secret Place

We knew our time in Tibet was coming to an end when one morning right after breakfast, a local Tibetan official brought a letter to our house. It was from the Chinese government who had found out we were living in Tibet without a visa.

"You must return to China immediately." The message was clear and to the point.

Daddy wrote back his reply the next day. "We are here sharing the gospel with the Tibetan people and need more time."

It was an outrageous move on Daddy's part. He figured if God had spoken to our hearts to go to Tibet, then the government would comply also. As for me, I began to fervently pray that God would not let this backfire on us. Standing up to a foreign government was not my kind of personality...or faith. If it were me, I would have found the next caravan going back into China and made sure I was on it.

But as strange as it seems, the government was not angry. They didn't give us a permanent visa but wrote back that we could have six more months. It was amazing. Visas into Tibet were rare, almost impossible to get and here we were receiving permission to stay longer. We knew God was with us and had given us favor and so we kept on working; passing out tracts, and witnessing everywhere we went.

One day while in prayer, Daddy began to pray for countries at war with each other. He began naming some of them: Germany, France, Italy, etc. It sounded preposterous to both of us. He stopped in the middle of his prayer, almost embarrassed at what was coming out of his mouth. We had not received any world news since we had been in Tibet, but without knowing it at the time, God was informing us of the World War that was breaking out even while we were up in those high, isolated mountains.

When we returned to China we found out that Daddy's prayers were coming to pass. It was if the Almighty had read the headlines of an international newspaper. I never get over being amazed at the Holy Spirit's ability to communicate with his children.

Meanwhile the bombing had escalated in China and the American Consulate was ordering all Americans to return home. "If you stay here, we will not be responsible for the safety of your family." He was stern and to the point. We knew he was right. All around us the Chinese were dying. Everyday thousands were killed. It was the beginning of great trouble and persecution for the Chinese church. There was still so much to be done, but we knew God was telling us to leave China. It seemed as if we were just getting started and neither Daddy nor I wanted to return home.

Our hearts were heavy as we packed up our few belongings, told our friends good-bye and boarded the train for the long journey back to Hong Kong. We knew something was wrong when minutes later, brakes screeching, the train came to an abrupt stop. Evidently no one knew that the tracks in front of us had been bombed the night before. Pandemonium and fear broke out all around us with hundreds of people grabbing children and belongings, running to get to another train. The possibility of being stranded was very real.

I noticed that wooden boxes were lined up on each side of the train tracks and wondered out loud at what they could be.

We hurried the children off the train, grabbed our bags, and started following the crowd to another train. I noticed that wooden boxes were lined up on each side of the train tracks and wondered out loud at what they could be.

"Those are caskets," someone answered my question.

I was horrified at the number of them and grieved for what they represented: hundreds of spouses, fathers and mothers, sisters and brothers violently separated from each other forever. We stepped past the dead bodies soberly, grateful that every one of us was alive and well. War was no longer just in the newspapers but right in front of us on every hand.

I wept for our Chinese friends, for all the people who died, for this beautiful land torn apart by a war they didn't even understand. Who ever understands war? What makes people kill each other? As for Daddy and the children and me, we were walking in Psalm ninety-one:

> *A thousand may fall at your side,*
> *And ten thousand at your right hand;*
> *But it shall not come near you…*
> *Because you have made the Lord who is my refuge,*
> *Even the Most High your dwelling place,*
> *No evil shall befall you.*

Everything you want from God is found through learning how to abide in Him. There is a secret place in God where His intimacy is all you will ever need and all you really want. When you start seeking that one thing and making time to sit in His presence, you will discover that everything else is provided for including safety and guidance.

You know you have found God's hiding place, when the peace you have in laying down your life for the sake of the gospel, is the same as the peace you need for living it for His glory. I believe there is a place in God where He is so near that either way is just fine. God calls it His secret place.

"He who dwells in the secret place of the Most High shall abide under the shadow of the Almighty. I will say of the Lord, He is my refuge and my fortress, My God in Him I will trust." (Psalm 91: 1, 2)

Chapter Thirty

Wisdom Is...Recognizing the Sound of His Footsteps

Getting back on the ship that would take us to the United States was a bittersweet experience. We were sorry we were leaving China, but made up our mind we would come back as soon as the war was over. The luxury of an ocean liner was a far cry from the life we had been living. For days I shook my head in wonder, trying to adjust to the wonderful meals that were being laid out before us. Food we had forgotten about—steak, mashed potatoes, cakes and pies—was plentiful and the children thought they were in heaven! Just a few days before, we had been rolling barley grains to dip into our hot buttered tea.

We had two rooms on the ship, one for Daddy and me and our baby, born in Tibet; and one for the other four children. Of course, the cabins were very small, just big enough for a bunk bed with a small porthole in each room. I told the children that there was no way around it—we were going to be living in very cramped quarters for twenty-one days.

One night I woke up to the sounds of a fierce storm outside and to the rocking and rolling of the ship inside. The lightning that sliced the blackness of the night was accompanied by large blasts of thunder that filled our small room and made the baby cry. I looked out the porthole to see a black angry sea with waves that were heaving us up and down like a toy boat in river rapids.

Fear immediately gripped me. "Are we going to survive this?" I wondered. I thought of my children in the next room and knew they must be scared if they were awake. Just getting out of bed was difficult and walking upright to get to them was almost impossible. *Had we come this far, through all of the dangers of war and hunger, to die in the middle of the night on a black angry sea?*

"God," I cried. "Please help us!"

As quick as the lightning flashing across the black sky, I heard the words of a scripture I had memorized during my devotions: "His footsteps are on the deep."

Peace was a sweet relief and I actually smiled at the picture that verse created in my mind. No wonder everything was rocking and rolling out there. That was God walking on the waters! Isn't it funny how the way we look at our circumstances can affect everything in just a moment's time? Because of a simple Bible verse filled with power, I could envision God, great and majestic and in control, so large that when He speaks the waves calm down. And when He decides to take a walk in the middle of the night, all of heaven and earth tremble at the power of His footsteps.

There is great wisdom in tucking the Word of God in our hearts. All manner of storms are a part of our journey from earth to glory, but with the Word guiding us through that dark night, we discover that God is with us even when we can't see Him. That rumbling noise you hear coming towards you is really God's footsteps walking on top of those deep, black waters. He is walking toward you—the apple of His eye.

"The waters saw you, O God; the waters saw you, they were afraid;
The depths also trembled, the clouds poured out water.
The skies sent out a sound; your arrows also flashed about.
The voice of your thunder was in the whirlwind,
the lightning lit up the world;
The earth trembled and shook. Your way was in the sea.
Your path in the great waters, and your footsteps were not known…"

(Psalms: 77: 16 – 19)

CHAPTER THIRTY-ONE

Wisdom is...Never Looking Back

From the moment we returned to the States from China and Tibet, all we thought about was how and when to get back into China. We knew that the war couldn't last forever and our desire to live out the rest of our days ministering to the Chinese people was as strong as ever. But while we were in the States, we did what we had always done— travel and preach wherever God opened the doors.

After six years of waiting for China to open back up, we decided to start making our way back to Asia by going to the Hawaiian Islands and wait for an opportunity to return. We decided we could serve God among the different people-groups living in the islands while we waited for our visas. Not only were there Japanese, Chinese, Filipinos, and Polynesians who needed the gospel, many of the American soldiers from the Mainland were still stationed on the islands. It was a fertile mission field and would also be our waiting room while we prepared to move back into China.

While we were in Honolulu, Daddy and I had our ninth child—Mary Elizabeth. She was one of the few of our children who were born in a hospital. This was the first time in years that I had a *real* doctor helping me give birth. He told me I was in excellent condition and obviously had excellent care with my many pregnancies.

I smiled, thinking how shocked he would be if I told him where and how all those babies had been born and that this was the first time I had been in a hospital or received a doctor's care since my first child. "I've been in very good hands," I told him truthfully.

By now we were all used to moving and starting over in a new place. The children especially were little troopers, adjusting to wherever Daddy and I took them. Not that Hawaii was difficult to get used to! Everywhere we went we saw beautiful hibiscus, ginger plants, palm trees, and pineapple fields. We were a long way from the harsh winters of Idaho and Montana and we were convinced that we had found the spot nearest heaven in Hilo, Hawaii.

We had found a big house right on the beach where the children had everything their hearts desired. They swam in the ocean, played on the beach, and ate raw sugar cane from the island's plantations. It was a child's dream. Daddy found a used, surplus army jeep so we packed the kids inside and drove around the island every day passing out tracts and holding services. Wherever we found people, whether in town or on the beach, we stopped to tell them about Jesus and how they could be saved.

Each of our children played a different instrument and we had our own little band wherever we went: accordion, ukulele, banjo, and trumpet. That always got a crowd! We sang songs while people gathered around, eager to be entertained. After we had their interest, Daddy preached about Jesus.

Daddy started to preach after Juanita and Danny had given their testimony, someone hollered out, "We don't want to hear you, we want to hear your children."

Of course the children would have much preferred to play all day, but we made sure that they participated in all of our outreaches. They always knew they were a part of the ministry. In fact, in Hawaii they learned how to be bold and speak to strangers about the Lord. One time when Daddy started to preach after Juanita and Danny had given their testimony, someone hollered out, "We don't want to hear you, we want to hear your children."

I guess it was far more interesting to listen to children speak about Jesus. The truth was that our children had seen the Lord heal us, provide for us, protect us, and guide us each step of the way. Every day we studied the Bible together and most evenings were spent in a church service somewhere. Even at such young ages their faith in God was strong and they knew more about the Lord than our listeners. I was proud of them for being bold and sharing their testimony of God's faithfulness.

One day, Daddy came in the house and abruptly announced that we were moving.

"Oh no," I thought to myself. "Here we go again. Just when everything is settled and the children and I are happy, Daddy has to start getting itching feet."

"Why?" I asked him. I couldn't understand this abrupt change of plans. Our home was open and airy and clean. We even had room for church services in the living room and besides, the children were so content. Everything seemed perfect to me.

"Because God said so," was his reply.

Just like that. No more reasoning than "God said so." By now I knew it was useless to argue with Daddy...or God. I sighed, w*ell Celia, just start packing and don't waste your breath arguing with either of them.* I knew that Daddy wouldn't change his mind. And if it was really God talking to him, well, *He* sure wasn't going to change *His* mind.

"Where are we going to move?" I asked Daddy, afraid of the answer.

"There's a nice little house near the Japanese village," he told me.

My heart sank. I knew the area he was talking about and it wasn't half as nice as where we were. When he showed me the house I felt sick. It was on stilts with only a few small bedrooms for our whole family. Compared to where we had been living, it was a shanty.

When we moved our family into our new house, I decided not to grumble or complain. Not that there weren't plenty of times that I wanted to! The rooms were small with an "open-air" kitchen, which was enclosed with loosely woven latticework that did little to keep out bugs and mosquitoes. Lizards and rats ran across the floors and ceilings and we had to sleep on the floor with mosquito nets tucked under the blankets.

One day while I was sweeping the kitchen I slipped and fell and my foot went straight through the floor! Termites had eaten through the wood and we soon discovered their handiwork everywhere. We learned to be careful when we walked inside the house and to never lean up against the walls.

At night when the children were asleep and the house was quiet, I poured out my complaint to the Lord privately. "Lord! I can't stand this. What is this about? Why would You tell us to move out of our nice home? Am I never to have anything comfortable and nice?" My resolve not to complain was weakening and I was having a hard time bending my will to match His. Obviously, if He had told me to move from a shanty to a nice house I would not have questioned Him, but I was having serious doubts as to whether Daddy had heard the voice of God.

Dear God! Our whole family would have been swept away while we were sleeping.

Just a few nights later, I heard the roar of what sounded like hundreds of jet engines revving up at one time. To this day I cannot tell you what a frightening sound that was. Daddy and I knew something terrible was happening, but we had no idea what. We decided to stay tucked in our little house with the children instead of venturing outside into the dark night to investigate. Prayer seemed like the better option.

The next morning we got up before dawn and went down to the sea to the area where we had heard the explosion. I had never seen the ocean so angry. Instead of the beautiful, lapping waves that we were used to, white foamy water was churning and crashing onto the beach. The whole ocean looked like some kind of sea-monster, still foaming mad.

We looked around for the house we had lived in but couldn't find it. Up on the hill, near the spot where it had been, we saw a little grandmother and her husband with their small grandchild sitting together, staring at the ocean in a dazed silence.

When we asked them what had happened, they described skyscraper high waves that went out to sea and came back, picked up our house and took it out to sea. I felt the hairs on my arm tingle. *Dear God! Our whole family would have been swept away while we were sleeping.* It would have been impossible to move all nine of our children to safety in the short amount of time that it took those waves to go out and come back again.

Forgive me, Lord, I immediately prayed. Even though I hadn't complained, I had questioned God and doubted Daddy's ability to hear God's voice. It was another one of those times when I learned first-hand about the importance and safety of submission.

Later I learned that the tidal wave actually began as an earthquake in Alaska and sent waves across the Pacific at the speed of a jet liner. It arrived in Hilo, Hawaii where we were living, just five hours later.

April 1, 1946, the day our family home was carried out to sea, is a historical date in Hawaii's history. That day 159 people were killed and 26 million dollars worth of damage was done by that tidal wave. In fact, that area where we used to live has been turned into a national park, a memorial to the destruction that cost so many Hawaiians their lives. For me, that park is a memorial to God's faithfulness in sparing the lives of the Dodge family.

When the word we hear from God is painful and hard, it is wise to remember that disobedience or even delayed obedience costs more in the long run. When we make decisions based on our comfort level, instead of the will of God, we will always pay a high price. Far better to move quickly and refuse to pine for what is no longer ours. When God speaks to you, do it and don't look back.

"Flee for your lives! Don't look back, and don't stop anywhere in the plain. Flee to the mountains or you will be swept away. ...But Lot's wife looked back, and she became a pillar of salt." (Genesis 19: 17, 26)

CHAPTER THIRTY-TWO

Wisdom is…Admitting We Don't Have All the Answers

Our time in Hawaii was a time of miraculous provision and beautiful surroundings, but it wasn't China, and China was where our hearts were. Month after month we waited, believing that any day God would open the doors for us to return to resume our ministry. But three years later we were still waiting.

Daddy and I both were faced with troubling questions. Hadn't we heard from God? Why didn't He stop us from starting out if He knew we couldn't get back into China? What about those times before when He miraculously provided a visa? Couldn't He do it again? Were we out of His will?

We began to fast and pray for God to show us whether we were to stay in the islands or return to the States. We were both discouraged. The heavens seemed to be made of cement, blocking our every petition. It seemed like God had left us alone and forgotten where we were.

I knew Daddy's faith was low when one day he said, "Momma, you pray for us. I don't trust myself to hear from God on this one. I don't know what we're supposed to do."

Now, this was hard for him to admit. Most of the time he was sure what our next step should be and he never hesitated. But now it seemed it was up to me to hear the voice of God for our next move. I prayed and fasted and prayed some more. I prayed in the morning and I prayed at night when the children were asleep but no matter how hard I prayed I couldn't get an answer.

What were we supposed to do? My heart was telling me to return to the Mainland, but I wasn't sure if those were my desires or God's will for us. What if

China's doors opened but we were not ready to go because we had returned home?

One night in a dream, I saw a long line of green lights. Nothing else. Just green lights as long and as far as I could see. I woke up in the morning and knew God had finally spoken. He was giving us the green light to go home. When I told Daddy about the dream he immediately agreed. "We're going home, then." We began to pack our bags and make preparation to return to the States.

Now, from my vantage point of many added years and experiences, I understand that life doesn't fit in neat, pretty boxes with perfect answers. When I was younger, I didn't understand that truth, and many times I thought I had failed God because things didn't turn out the way I planned. Now I know that not all prayers are answered when and how I want them to be answered and not all problems have great endings—even when we are seeking God with all of our heart.

To this day, I don't know why God didn't open the doors to China. But I figure it was just another opportunity to trust Him with everything in my life, even the unanswered questions.

It's all right to ask questions. God knows they are in our hearts. But we also have to be prepared to trust Him when we don't have all the answers. Admitting to ourselves and to people around us that we don't have solutions to our own dilemma is a very humbling experience.

None of us hear the voice of God perfectly. During those times, the sacrifice that we can give God is a humble attitude that acknowledges that He is God and His ways are higher than ours. Trusting Him when He is silent is a mark of spiritual maturity.

"For now we see in a mirror, dimly, but then face to face. Now I know in part, but then I shall know just as I also am known." (I Corinthians 13: 12)

CHAPTER THIRTY THREE

Wisdom is...Leaving a Heritage of Faith

A documentary called "Black Gold" about the people of Africa, literally changed my life. For the first time in my life, I saw pictures of the Nupe tribe, a people who carved the flesh of their children's faces to identify them as belonging to the same family-group. For months afterwards I found myself praying for them.

Since our time in China, Daddy and I had settled into ministering to churches in the States and even though we had made several trips into Mexico to preach the gospel, it was not enough for me. I have always loved missions and taught my children to love missions and I wanted to be on the "front lines" again. I told God He could send me to Africa if He needed me to go.

Daddy didn't seem interested when I talked to him about what I was feeling in my heart and I didn't press the matter. Instead, I tucked my desire away and began to pray that if it was God's will for us to go that He would open the doors. Several years passed and nothing happened, but I kept praying anyway.

One day I was sitting in a bus station waiting for the next bus and noticed several people stepping on a scale to check their weight. All of them put their dime into the machine, read their weight, and then picked up a little ticket that came out of the machine. I must have been bored because I was curious to know what those little notes said. I got up and weighed myself and picked up my pink piece of paper *"You will go abroad in your later years,"* the ticket read. I laughed at myself, thinking how silly of me to get excited about a little piece of paper. "Yes Lord, I'm going abroad." I prayed right there, still standing in front of the scales. Now you and I both know that God would not use a set of scales with silly little forecasts to talk to you. Or would He?

I thought back to that documentary on Africa and knew there had to be a reason that I could not get that continent out of my heart or mind. I didn't need a piece of paper to tell me that I was going abroad, but the question was, when? I began to pray more fervently than ever. It was time to talk to Daddy again. When I told him how I had been praying for several years that God would send us to Africa, he was surprised but not convinced that God was speaking to me.

"Well, if it's God, He will supply the need," was Daddy's response to the matter. I could tell by the tone of his voice that he was dismissing it as an unlikely possibility. We both knew it would take thousands of dollars for us to pay for the fares to Africa, and then there was monthly support to raise on top of that.

Still I knew that if it was of the Lord we would go. All I had to do was be quiet and let God talk to Daddy and lead us out into His will. I thought back to the days when we were faced with the same kind of need when we felt the Lord speak to us to go to China. If He supplied a miracle then, He could do it again.

I laid all of my desires on the altar. "Now, Lord," I prayed, "I am willing to go to Africa, but you are going to have to work in Daddy's heart and supply the money to go.

I reasoned that if I did my part, which was preparing my heart to do the will of God, then it was up to Him to take care of the rest.

The first miracle was that Daddy began to pray and ask God if we should go. He was not going to make such drastic moves based on what God was telling me...he had to hear it from God first-hand. But I knew I had planted a seed in his mind and he was not going to rest until he knew what we should do. He began to tell people that we were "thinking" of going to Africa.

The second miracle happened several months later at a conference we were attending. One of the pastors, a close friend of ours, walked up to Daddy between teaching sessions and said, "I have six thousand dollars for your fare to Africa whenever you're ready to go."

That was it. We were on our way. Neither Daddy nor I could deny that God was leading us to go to Nigeria. We were launching out again to a new

———— ¶ ————

One of the pastors…

said, "I have six

thousand dollars

for your fare

to Africa whenever

you're ready to go."

land where the people and customs, language, and food would all be strange. But both of us had pioneer spirits and loved the challenge. Once again we packed up our belongings and headed out to worlds unknown, at least to us.

Once we arrived in Africa, I immediately felt at home and knew that we were exactly where God wanted us to be. Learning to live in this new land though was another matter altogether. The Lord knows I wasn't used to luxury in the States, but I still missed the basics: electricity, fans, and refrigeration. The local market was full of flies and filth with pungent smells that took our breath away. Once a week the local butchers slaughtered a cow. Every Wednesday morning we rushed to the market to buy our beef before the afternoon sun took its toll on the large slabs of meat hanging on hooks from the ceiling.

We lived in a large compound with forty African evangelists and pastors who came from the surrounding area for three months of Bible training. Our daily schedule was a routine that we quickly settled into: classes until noon, a break in the hot part of the day, and then out into the bush for evangelistic meetings at night.

I don't believe I have ever been happier than those days in Ikot, Nigeria. *This is what I was born for*, I remember thinking to myself. There is nothing as satisfying to me as helping people and sharing the gospel, and in Africa I was doing both.

Neither Daddy nor I minded the harsh living conditions, but we were not prepared for the malaria attacks that weakened our bodies. Daddy was much sicker than I was and seemed to have a harder time recovering from the high fever and pain that wracked his body. At the end of our first year in Africa, he was completely depleted of physical stamina and spiritual strength. It was obvious that we had to return to the States for a time of recuperation. After a time of rest, we returned to Nigeria but he became seriously ill again. The doctor told him he should go home and stay there—his body could not take any more malaria attacks.

When we returned home near the end of the year, we had established twenty-five churches. The Lord had given us a team of African men who loved God, loved the Word, and had a vision for their own people. We knew we couldn't leave them stranded when we left so we supported them from the States, making sure they had what they needed to continue the work. Their needs were really simple: a bicycle to get around on, a lantern for the dark nights in the bush, and a battery operated P.A. system for the villages they ministered in.

...nothing could make me happier than to know that the love God planted in my heart for Africa thirty-five years ago is still living in my grandchildren.

Leaving our friends and co-workers broke my heart. I would have been happy to live out the rest of my days in Africa. But that wasn't what God wanted me to do, so I bowed my will to His again. Five of my eleven children have ministered in Africa and a few years ago one of my grandsons, who is a pastor in Houston, Texas, went back to visit some of the churches we started.

"Grandma, I feel I'm going to go back there to live someday," he told me not too long ago. For me, nothing could make me happier than to know that the love God planted in my heart for Africa thirty-five years ago is still living in my grandchildren.

It is a sobering thought to realize that decisions we make today are affecting future generations. When you and I obey God, we are handing a heritage of righteousness to our seed's seed…even those who haven't been born yet.

On the other hand, the choices we make that are contrary to wisdom and God's plan for our lives can leave scars for years to come. That's why it is so important that we walk out our days in the fear of the Lord.

"For none of us lives to himself, and no one dies to himself."

(Romans 14:7)

CONCLUSION

ENDURING TO THE END

Enduring To The End

It doesn't seem like I should be ninety-two already. My spirit still feels young but my body, well that's another story—it just doesn't seem to obey me much these days. I find myself thinking of heaven more often now. I actually get happy when I think of that moment when I will see Jesus face-to-face. More than ever before, I am convinced that the most important thing in the world for you and me is to keep the faith and endure to the end.

That isn't always easy. I remember the time in my life when I thought my life wasn't worth living and considered ending it in the dark waters of a swirling river near our house. About a year after Daddy and I were married, I realized that I was married to a man who was as different from me as night was from day. Before the wedding, it never dawned on me that there would be any serious problems. We loved each other, didn't we? The only marriage I knew intimately was my mom and dad's, and they never argued or fussed. They always seemed happy to me. I just naturally thought that I would be happy, too.

But Daddy loved to drink and gamble and often came home drunk after spending the week's paycheck on liquor. Juanita Arlene, our first child, was a baby and I was horrified to think that she would grow up knowing that kind of life instead of the happy, carefree one I had as a child. When I realized that I couldn't change my husband, I despaired. *How could I live like this?* How could I raise my baby with a man who didn't stay home much and didn't seem to care about our needs? I was shocked and dismayed at how our lives were turning out and felt helpless and defeated.

One night I left the house, desperate. I didn't know where I was going but it didn't matter. I had to get away and decide what to do. My life was unbearable and I was at the end of myself.

I thought of my mother and father and how sad they would be to know the life style I was in. I couldn't tell them, of course. And I couldn't go back to them. I always knew that for better or for worse, marriage was forever. I had made my decision, and now I was stuck with it.

I walked down by the river, mesmerized by the black water. How does a thought get in your head? I don't know. But on that night, it seemed like the most logical thing in the world to jump in and let myself be swept away under the blanket of darkness. I was a nurse and knew better than anyone else that there was no painkiller for the despair that was in my heart. *Wouldn't it be better to just end it all?* My mind wavered back and forth on a seesaw of emotions trying to make what could be a final decision.

> *...it seemed like the most logical thing in the world to jump in and let myself be swept away under the blanket of darkness.*

I thought of the day I was baptized into the Lutheran church—I was ten years old, wearing a starched white pinafore dress, my black hair tightly woven in long braids down my back. I knew it was one of the most important days of my life and I listened to every word the preacher said. "Jesus died for you" was the title of his sermon and I immediately believed and accepted Jesus into my life. I was overwhelmed with a deep love for God and a longing to be with Him. All the way home I thought of how I could arrange to be with Him and finally came up with a simple solution; I would climb the windmill behind the house and jump into the arms of God. I wasn't afraid to die, only intent on being in heaven.

But now, I was afraid to live. I was still staring at the river, trying to make up my mind when I remembered my early days of Sunday school. It was a sin to take a life—even our own—the teacher had told us.

"I'll go to hell," I remember thinking. *What if it was worse than the one I was in?* It was one thing to want to jump from a windmill because I wanted to talk with God. It was quite another to jump into a swirling river because I wanted to escape life. I thought of my baby back home and the kind of life she would have without me. *What was I thinking?*

I walked back to our little one room apartment and picked my sweet little girl out of her cot. I knew I could never take an easy way out when my child needed me. Whatever the future held, I was going to walk into it. To this day, I don't believe I would have ever taken my life, but it was a strong thought. A temptation. I was in deep despair, but God was watching over me. I'm sure He could see the young girl in the confirmation dress and at the same time, He saw ahead to this day when, as a ninety-two-year-old woman, I still enjoy a rich life of friends and children and grandchildren and great-grandchildren.

> *Wouldn't the devil be happy if he could have changed the course of so many lives with one decision?*

It wasn't long after that terrible night by that black river that Daddy accepted Jesus and turned his life around. We had sixty-five rich years of being together that I would not trade for anything in the world.

The key to all of life is to never give up. Never give up on God…or your marriage…or your children…or God's will for you. When we are too weak to have strong faith, we can hold on to hope. Hope is really faith in disguise. When we can't see any change with our natural eye, hope will keep our eyes on Jesus. I've known deep sadness since that time, but I have never been without hope. I learned that God's grace is equal to whatever happens. Hope is part of our salvation and I still draw on it often.

"Just think," I tell my children today, "what if I had jumped in those waters and given up. Wouldn't the devil be happy if he could have changed the course of so many lives with one decision?"

What are you waiting for God to change in your life? Be patient and hope in the Lord. It will happen, just like He promised it would. But if you give up before it happens, I ask you, is that God's fault?

The key to everything is to endure. And sometimes when your heart or body is full of pain, the end seems like a long way away. That's why people give up. Sometimes we lose hope because we are tired of the responsibilities of life that never seem to end.

I remember when Daddy and I were doing mission work in Hawaii, a minister that we both respected came to visit. He was a father in-the-faith and a veteran minister. He had a wealth of experience and wisdom and we often sought counsel from him.

I was busy with all the usual "mother" things: cooking, washing clothes, cleaning, and watching over a house of very active children. I had to excuse myself several times while we were visiting to check on the pot of soup on the stove and to make sure the smaller children who were playing in the yard were all right.

When I re-entered the conversation, he addressed his words to me and crushed my spirit.

"You know, Sister Dodge, you aren't a real missionary. Brother Dodge is the missionary of the family. You're a wife and mother."

I kept a smile on my face and didn't reply, but that night after tucking the children in bed, I cried out my anguish to God. All I had ever

Without knowing it, I was raising ministers that would impact the world.

wanted to do was to preach the gospel and be a missionary. "Is he right?" I asked God. A wave of hopelessness swept over me. *Was all the hard work for nothing?*

I look back at that time now and realize how mistaken that minister was. Not only were Daddy and I ministering together, but I was impacting eternity with every diaper I washed and every meal I cooked. Without knowing it, I was raising ministers that would impact the world.

A few months ago, I was feeling very discouraged with my body, which seems to get tired more often these days and hinders my vision to keep working for God.

"Mother, you are spreading the gospel through your children now: in Irian Jaya through Faith, in Russia through Paul, in Washington D.C. through Amos," my daughter started naming my children and their ministries. She reminded me of Japan where my grandchildren worked as missionaries and established churches, and of Thailand where there is a girl's home because of our family. Oregon…Texas…Florida…North Carolina…Montana…she named the states where my children and grandchildren have established churches and ministries.

By the time she was through, I felt encouraged and lighthearted again. It's true. The seed of faith that was planted in my children through day in and day out living keeps multiplying throughout the world in countless other lives.

The way you and I will change this world is by staying faithful to whatever God has called us to do. Perseverance…endurance…patience…longsuffering… they are all different words describing our faith. If we are wise, we will not let anything ensnare our hearts or minds—or steal our faith.

The greatest joy I've had in life is sharing the gospel of Christ and watching people get saved.

Now that I'm getting close to the end, I am convinced of one thing: there is nothing like doing the will of God. The greatest joy I've had in life is sharing the gospel of Christ and watching people get saved. Not too long ago, I asked my friend, Gail, to take me to a prison not far from my home. I wanted to share my faith with someone who needed hope. A young man gave his heart to the Lord and it made me so happy I felt new energy for days. That's the way it works. When you pour yourself into the souls of men, God pours into you.

The Bible clearly tells us that dark times will come upon the earth. The world seems to be getting more wicked all the time and we Christians are the only ones who can stop the onslaught of sin. In fact, the Bible says that darkness will cover the earth, but the glory of the Lord will come upon us. I believe you and I will keep shining as lights in a dark world. No matter what happens, there is nothing to be afraid of. Just stand up and be counted until the end. Take a stand for truth and see what happens.

We are all on the shortest part of a journey that will go on for all eternity. I'm getting closer to the day when Daddy and I will be together again, both of us bowing low before the Throne where our King reigns forever. I know I will see His Glory and that makes everything worthwhile. I have seen the rewards of endurance and plan to keep right on believing and hoping until the very end.

Our Leah's Sister's team had just completed a ministry trip to the women of Kenya and Rwanda, Africa, and were in the Nairobi International Airport on our way home when I realized the unthinkable: my ticket home was missing. Heart pounding, I went through my handbag, carry-on, and suitcases, my belongings sprawled out in the middle of the busy airport. I could feel the disdainful and pitying stares of the people around me. I recognized the smug satisfaction that I had felt myself while standing behind some poor, pitiful soul at the ticket counter who obviously didn't have their act together. Lost luggage might be a failure of an airline, but missing tickets or passports spoke of the unorganized and inexperienced. An international traveler for most of my life, I was chagrined that such a thing was actually happening to me.

A frantic call to the hotel where we had stayed produced nothing. " It happens sometimes that tickets are stolen," was the nonchalant comment from the manager. "Check with the police."

I choked back tears of frustration as my friends and I drove to the Nairobi police station to report a missing ticket. I knew the procedure was probably futile but necessary if I were to convince the airlines to issue a new one. A copy of the report in hand, we tried to look confident while marching up to the Northwest Airlines ticket counter, pleading for mercy.

None was given. Obviously, I was not going to leave Nairobi without more paperwork and days of negotiating with the airline officials.

There was nothing to do but send the team back home while I worked with the powers that be for a few days in an attempt to recover the hundreds of dollars that the missing ticket represented. Thanksgiving was three days away and I had promised Mother I would be out at the Texas ranch with her to celebrate it, but there was no way around it. I was going to experience a Nairobi Thanksgiving. On my own.

"Mary, would you buy me a coke?" It was Kim, my associate, asking me for a favor. I swallowed some well-appointed words on timing and selfishness and walked across the airport looking for a coke machine, regretting all the lessons I had taught on servant leadership, maturity and humility. Did the woman have no sensitivity at all?

When I returned to the desk, she triumphantly held up a new ticket, offering that it was a gift from her, that if I didn't go home, no one would and that yes, she was too smart to think I would allow her to do it, thus the immediate need for a coke.

A few days later, still in jet lag, I was sitting in my aged Mother's living room, happy that I had been able to keep my promise to her. Thanksgiving dinner was over, the dishes done, the family scattered back to their homes when my brother returned to Mom's house to deliver the unthinkable news: my older brother Jake had died in Idaho that afternoon. While waiting for Thanksgiving dinner, he had decided to use his "cherry picker" to trim a few of the trees on his property overlooking Lake Coeur d' Alene. The equipment slipped on some rocks and he fell to his death.

...the dishes done, the family scattered back to their homes when my brother returned to Mom's house to deliver the unthinkable news...

I crawled into bed with Mother that night and cradled her in my arms while we both cried together. Her pain was different than mine...this was her child, the first one out of eleven that she had lost and perhaps the one who brought her the most comfort. Jake was a successful businessman and besides providing for his wife and children, he made sure Mother never wanted for anything. He flew across the States to visit her often and called her often, "just to make sure everything was okay." He knew when her water pipes were frozen, what her telephone bill was, what medicines she needed. He arranged family reunions, flying in her children from around the States, giving her the gift that for Mom, was above all others—her kids all together at one place at the same time. For Mom, Jake was her strength in old age. She loved all of us, but leaned on Jake.

We laid there in the dark, mother dozing off and on, intermittently crying and praying, " Why, Lord? I don't understand." Groans in her sleep said the grief had penetrated her subconsciousness and was hurting her all over.

How strange and fragile—life. Here was a ninety-two-year-old woman, frail with age, grieving the life of a robust son who should have been at her funeral. Mother was at the door of eternity, a long, full life behind her, yet one last great grief to suffer before stepping out of the "vale of tears" the old hymn talks about. It seemed unfair. I cried for her, for Jake's wife and children, for all of us. Indeed. "Why, Lord?"

...this moment would be one of my most cherished for the rest of my life.

Grief seems more intense, more black and hopeless at night. I wanted to keep vigil over Mom until the morning but despaired that it would ever come. A mixture of jet lag and shock kept me staring into the darkness while agonizing minutes refused to move into hours. Finally, toward the morning light, I could hear Mother praying again. Only one word, spoken over and over, it came out as a pain filled cry.

"Yes," she was saying. "Yes." A few minutes would pass and I could hear her again, "Yes. Yes, Lord."

Sometimes memories don't become great until they've aged, but I knew laying beside my aged hero that Thanksgiving night, that this moment would be one of my most cherished for the rest of my life. In my all-night grief vigil with Mom, she had taught me one of the greatest lessons about life that I would ever learn. In fact, I didn't know which plan God had in mind when he expedited my return trip from Nairobi; for me to be with Mother to comfort her on this Thanksgiving Day— or for Mom to teach me another life lesson that I desperately needed.

The stooped, wrinkled body with the wobbly feet and poor hearing housed a great, strong spirit that had matured through a life of accepting the unexpected on this cradle-to-the-grave journey. Mom had mastered the art of getting from the "why" to "yes" in the least possible amount of time.

...it was one of those "hardest-things-I've-ever-done" milestones in my life.

Yes, life is hard. And evidently, it doesn't get easier. I learned from Momma that you can live a godly life, get up to the last moments of it, put your first foot in the door of eternity, and still have to bear one last crushing blow. We live in a world where sin and disease, accidents and death happen to all of us. And always, it seems, when we least expect them. You can be a prayer warrior, a missionary, a giver of life and it still won't keep you from grief and pain. And yes, God help us, the first word that often comes out of our mouth is, "Why, Lord?" It's an honest question that never seems to offend an all-knowing Father.

But camping out at the "why" is dangerous. It's a question one must eventually release because of the bitterness and just-below-the-surface simmering kind of rage that hardens around the periphery of the soul with its overuse. Blame, guilt, and a kind of cool indifference toward God often follow.

Sometimes, in spite of our degree in theology, our life-wisdom, and training in psychology, there are no answers to the whys. Getting to the "yes" does not mean that we blithely accept shallow reasoning for the sake of a pacified soul. But rather that we walk out a strong trust in what we know about God in spite of the agonizing facts around us.

Later I would have opportunity to practice the wisdom of "yes" when releasing Mother to death's determined arms. In spite of months of preparation and praying the prayer of relinquishment, it was one of those "hardest things I've ever done" milestones in my life. (I've had more than one). I resented those trying to comfort me with the fact that Mother was ninety-two, full of age, ready to go. All true. But the fact of life is that you are never ready to let a mother walk out the door forever. Not even when you are in your fifties and she is in her nineties.

In the end I practiced prying open my fingers and letting her go. Faith walks on the stilts of grace and gets through the mountain of pain through the power of a the well-timed and often repeated "yes."

I learned that from Momma.

To order additional books contact:

Leah's Sisters
P.O. Box 17-1234
Irving, Texas,
75017-1234
Tel: 972.254.5004
Email: info@leahssisters.org

Or to order online:
www.leahssisters.org